Charles Dickens's London

Books by the same author

The Victorian Historical Novel 1840–1880
Charles Dickens: Resurrectionist
The Companion to A Tale of Two Cities
The Short Oxford History of English Literature
Anthony Trollope
Dickens and the Spirit of the Age
Authors in Context: Charles Dickens

Charles Dickens's London

Andrew Sanders

ROBERT HALE · LONDON

ISBN 978-0-7090-8831-8

Robert Hale Limited
Clerkenwell House
Clerkenwell Green
London EC1R 0HT

www.halebooks.com

A catalogue record for this book is available from the British Library

2 4 6 8 10 9 7 5 3 1

Typeset by e-type, Liverpool
Printed in China by Midas Printing international Ltd

Contents

The author would like to thank the Charles Dickens Museum,
in particular Florian Schweitzer, for their generous help
in providing many of the photographic illustrations.

Introduction

CHARLES DICKENS WAS not born in London, and the modest house in Portsmouth where he *was* born was so far from the sound of Bow Bells that he could never have laid claim to be a Cockney. However, unlike writers such as Milton or Byron, who were actually born in London, Dickens's literary achievement is inextricably associated with the metropolis. Their contemporaries might have been hard pressed to discover anything distinctively 'Londony' about Milton or Byron. Both were manifestly European men of letters and both aspired to be identified with a culture that stretched far beyond the confines of a single city, however large and influential that city might be. London was essentially incidental to their work. It was the centre of Dickens's.

Like certain other adopted literary Londoners, most notably Shakespeare and Dr Johnson, Dickens became identified with London because the great city served as a spur to his creativity and as an urban crucible. It was a crucible in which ideas and sensations, faces and voices were compounded. It was a place of assimilation and of experimentation. In London Shakespeare could meet the challenge presented by the work of rival play-wrights and he attracted to the Globe Theatre audiences drawn from a wide spectrum of Elizabethan and Jacobean society. Dr Johnson, who famously proclaimed, 'When a man is tired of London, he is tired of life', rejoiced in the society of his 'club' where writers mixed convivially with actors and painters. But Dickens was not merely stimulated by London and by his fellow Londoners. He consistently remade the city and its citizens in his work.

Charles Dickens. From a *carte-de-visite* photograph of the 1860s

John Keats, another London-born writer who only minimally deals with 'the matter of London' in his work, was accused by a singularly unsympathetic critic of being part of a 'Cockney school of poetry'. The critic did not necessarily believe that Keats's verse was characterized by dropped aitches and ungrammatical sentence structures, but that there was something essentially 'vulgar' about his style. The fact that the word 'Cockney' could have been used in this snobbish context in the early nineteenth century suggests that there existed a belief that an exclusively London-based literary scene was to be readily identified with vulgarity. What was implied was that a university-educated 'gentlemanly' writer, especially one ancestrally rooted in the provinces, would naturally eschew the taint of London streets and London sounds. London, it was held, was a city that could exercise a malign influence on the ill-bred and inexperienced writer, particularly one who had not been born into the upper classes. Take for example the distaste for London speech exhibited by the editor of Walker's *Pronouncing Dictionary* of 1791. Walker insists that Cockneys

> … have the disadvantage of being more disgraced by their peculiarities than any other people. The grand difference between the metropolis and the provinces is that people of education in London are generally free of the vices of the vulgar; but the best-educated people in the provinces, if consistently resident there, are sure to be tinctured with the dialect of the country in which they live. Hence it is that the vulgar pronunciation of London, though not half so erroneous as that of Scotland, Ireland, or any of the provinces, is, to a person of correct taste, a thousand times more offensive and disgusting.

Readers of the supposedly 'Cockney' Keats were warned to be on their guard against his likely lapses in taste and good literary manners. Significantly, Keats was not to draw his inspiration from the streets and by-ways of the city in which he had been born and bred. As a poet of his period he sought his inspiration in nature, in classical mythology and in medieval story-telling. Dickens, the adoptive Londoner, was, by contrast, to relish the stimuli that the city gave him. It was not just the London faces and places that stirred his imagination; he was also to rejoice in the very sounds of the streets and in the idiomatic speech of Londoners.

When Dickens first established his reputation as a writer in the late 1830s, great cities like London were manifestly redefining the received idea of culture. None of the established capitals of Europe was actually new, but the rapid growth in size, population and influence of cities like London or Paris was forcibly shifting perspectives about the nature of civilization. The refined culture associated with an academy, a royal court or aristocratic salons had declined. Generally, they had been eclipsed in a far less stratified urban world. The great city of the nineteenth century was both more complex and more socially and economically diverse. A city like London had, of course, always been predominantly the preserve of merchants and tradesmen, of bankers and shopkeepers, of lawyers and surgeons. It was also crowded with clerks and apprentices, with skilled craftsmen and unskilled labourers, with porters and dockers, with ferrymen and innkeepers, and with a multitude of domestic servants, both male and female. In the opening decades of the nineteenth century London was teeming with human life owing to an unprecedented growth in its population. It was also teeming with new ideas about the nature and constitution of society and about how art could best serve this new society.

By the opening years of the nineteenth century the patronage of literature in England had effectively shifted away from courts and salons. This was not because the upper classes had lost interest in 'high' culture and had given up any pretence of acting as arbiters of taste, but because the huge growth in literacy had broadened and challenged old social perspectives. The readership of books in general had vastly expanded, but the readership of the most popular variety, novels, had expanded particularly dramatically. Novels, and the audience for novels, were effectively classless. The steady rise of the novel during the eighteenth century may not always have been to the taste of the kind of critics who firmly maintained a belief in what was deemed to be the traditional supremacy of poetry over prose, but they were fighting a losing battle. At the beginning of the nineteenth century the vast popularity of Sir Walter Scott's novels seemed to prove that prose fiction could be both entertaining and educational. As the work of Scott's women contemporaries, Jane Austen, Frances Burney and Maria Edgeworth, also suggested, high-quality fiction was no longer the preserve of male writers. Victorian novelists readily recognized that there was a vast and growing public appetite for fiction.

A novel that proved a success with readers was also likely to prove a 'nice little earner'. As the nineteenth century developed, commercial considerations were often as significant as aesthetic ones in moulding the new generation of hopeful novelists who pestered publishers with their manuscripts. The Brontë sisters were not alone in seeking financial independence through novel writing.

Men with an intellectual axe to grind and women who had espoused a particular moral cause knew that a successful novel was more capable of influencing public opinion than a host of pamphlets. Once read, pamphlets were likely to gather dust; successful novels rarely remained the preserve of a single reader.

The very form of the novel made it more versatile than either poetry or non-fiction prose. As a rule novels told stories, and those stories, unlike the old romances, were likely to be concerned more with ordinary life than with fantasy. Any escapes from painful reality that novels offered were likely to be into another kind of reality. Novels could be predominantly love stories, or they could describe a character's earnest advance in the world to fame and fortune. They could be as readily set on a country estate as in a manufacturing city. They could be comic or veer towards tragedy. They could be deadly serious and weighed down with facts or they could light-heartedly seek to do nothing more than amuse. They could be elaborate historical costume dramas, or they could explore the drab niceties of life in a modern provincial town. Sometimes novels could be serious and funny at the same time. Above all, novels drew their characters from all stations in society and from all walks of life. As Scott's popular 'Waverley' novels served to suggest, the old heroics, the tribal battles and the weighty destinies of epic poetry, were generally tempered, and sometimes utterly banished, by an evocation of real people faced with real dilemmas. In the place of antique chivalry and the improbable love-making of the old pastorals, modern novels described everyday courtship and marriage, functional and dysfunctional families, economic and social aspiration, the commonplace rhythms of daily life and the domestic deathbed.

To a considerable degree the nineteenth century had to reinvent both its heroes and its concept of heroism. As Dickens's friend and mentor, Thomas Carlyle, told appreciative and responsive audiences in the London of the 1840s, even the man of letters had emerged as an heroic figure. The man of letters, and increasingly the woman of letters, had shrugged off a reliance on aristocratic patronage. They now relied on their literary earnings. These 'heroic' new writers had also freed themselves from the old aristocratic manners, tropes and prejudices which had once exclusively shaped literature. The success of a novel, as most Victorian readers would have recognized, was dependent neither on the good breeding of its author nor on the social assumptions of a narrow and socially exclusive audience. It was no longer based on an ability to please an elite but on what was potentially a mass readership.

In an important way, Charles Dickens, a writer of relatively obscure social origins but an upwardly mobile and ambitious self-made man, was the quintessential writer of his period. For many discriminating modern readers he remains the greatest of the English Victorian novelists and the one who best caught the spirit of the age. He knew very little about rural life, he was a 'townie' through and through, and from the middle years of his boyhood he knew London better than any other city. But instead of narrowing his scope as a writer his use of London in his novels gave him a distinctive variety and a very particular vitality. London, the greatest city of the age, made him articulate. It was not only fitting that he should have taken the life of London as his subject but, given the natural bent of his art, he could really have chosen no other city and no other subject.

Charles Dickens Museum

Borough High Street, c. 1900. A typical central London street as Dickens would have known it. The buildings date from the seventeenth to the early nineteenth centuries. Dickens would have known these buildings from the time of his boyhood

Cities had long provided artists with subjects. Cities, ancient and modern, were where social classes intermixed and where social hierarchies were challenged by urban circumstances. In important ways Latin literature had led the way. The ancient Roman writer, Petronius, set much of his comic masterpiece, *Satyricon*, in the imperial capital, and the work was to have a considerable, if belated, influence on the development of urban literature in England (though it only survives in a fragmentary form and those fragments did not become well known until the late seventeenth century). For the most part, *Satyricon* deals with low-life characters, with prostitutes, slaves, petty criminals and deviants, but it also famously describes the extravagances and the sexual and sensual appetites of the rich.

Dickens may well have been aware of *Satyricon* only as a semi-pornographic text but he was certainly aware of the models provided by other ancient comic writing. Through his profound acquaintance with the London comedies of the English seventeenth-century playwright, Ben Jonson, the most 'Roman' of all the contemporaries of Shakespeare, Dickens must have had some feel for the Latin tradition in which Jonson's work lay. It was Jonson who had most triumphantly reshaped the classical dramatic models established by the ancient playwrights Terence and Plautus. Jonson's London-based plays, such as *Everyman in his Humour*, *Bartholomew Fair* and *The Alchemist*, had a ready appeal to the actor and playwright *manqué* in Dickens. *Bartholomew Fair* and *The Alchemist* in particular are linked to precise London locations which lay close to the theatres where the plays were first performed. In 1845 Dickens and some of his literary friends mounted a celebrated amateur production of *Everyman in his Humour* (Dickens played the bombastic Captain Bobadil 'with an air of supreme conceit and frothy pomp'). Two years later the novelist was cast as the extravagantly verbose Sir Epicure Mammon in a proposed production of *The Alchemist*, but alas this particular revival of the play was abandoned after only two rehearsals.

The precedent represented by Jonson's London comedies remained familiar to writers and artists in the century that preceded Dickens's birth. Eighteenth-century London dominated the tastes, the values and the vices of a prosperous, self-confident and imperial Britain, but Jonson's gulls, fools, hypocrites and ambitious get-rich-quickers remained familiar enough to latter-day audiences. The dark underbelly of London life was not only the stuff of comedy. George Lillo's hugely popular domestic tragedy of 1731, *The London Merchant, or the History of George Barnwell*, told the harrowing moral story of a City apprentice who is seduced and corrupted by an unscrupulous courtesan and who goes on to steal from his worthy employer and to murder a rich uncle in his garden in suburban Camberwell. After agonizing over his sins in the condemned cell at Newgate, Barnwell is finally hanged for his crime at Tyburn. Dickens had seen this once stock item in the repertories of eighteenth- and nineteenth-century theatres as a boy in Rochester and he was to describe Mr Wopsle's wearisome reading of the play in Chapter 15 of *Great Expectations* (at the end of which Mr Pumblechook pointedly remarks to Pip: 'Take warning, boy, take warning').

Lillo's tragedy almost certainly influenced the moral tone of William Hogarth's famous series of engravings of 'Industry and Idleness' (also known as 'The Idle and Industrious Apprentice'), with which Dickens was very familiar. Hogarth's images are echoed in the work of the eighteenth-century novelists that Dickens most admired, Henry Fielding and Tobias Smollett. They were also the artists from whom he learned much of his craft as a writer. Both had chosen to set significant episodes in their fiction in a vibrant London where loose morals, political sleaze and manifest temptation are rife. David Copperfield, in the midst of his boyhood misery, finds solace and imaginative stimulus in the work of both novelists (though he coyly admits that he was too naïve to pick up the sexual overtones in Fielding's greatest work, having been 'a child's Tom Jones, a harmless creature'). Later in the novel, when David is at school, he retells the story of Smollett's *Peregrine Pickle* to the sleepless Steerforth.

Dickens's biographer, John Forster, was to suggest that *Peregrine Pickle* was a direct influence on *Pickwick Papers* in that both Peregrine and Mr Pickwick suffer a period of confinement in the Fleet Prison. Prisons were, of course, to loom darkly in Dickens's imagination. The concluding third of Fielding's *Tom Jones* is set in a London in which the world of fashion sits awkwardly next to a darker world of petty crime, corruption and the horrors attendant on destitution. It is in London that Lady Bellaston and Lord Fellamar connive at Tom's arrest and imprisonment. A similar contrast of elegance and squalor, good manners and unscrupulousness, virtue and recklessness characterizes Fielding's later novel, *Amelia*. This novel includes a particularly harrowing account of the filthy and dehumanizing condition of Newgate Prison, something that Fielding must have drawn from his experiences as a London magistrate. Such was Dickens's admiration for Fielding and his work that he named his sixth son Henry Fielding Dickens in his honour.

Dickens's novels differ from those of Smollett and Fielding in

The Fleet Prison, Fleet Market (now Farringdon Street), 1811. This water-colour by George Shepherd shows the debtors' prison where Mr Pickwick was incarcerated. The Fleet was closed in 1842 and its inmates transferred to the Queen's (late King's) Bench Prison in the Borough. The old buildings were demolished in 1845–6

that London itself takes on something of a character. The city no longer simply provides a background to the action, it is part of the essence of the action. The eighteenth-century 'comic' novelists had begun to explore the dark side of the city, but they had used London as a setting and little more. The metropolis had served largely as a mere aspect of what they had developed: a flexible, multi-plot, multi-character narrative. It was for Dickens, with a vastly sprawling and teeming London before him, to transform the shape of the Georgian novel into an art form capable of reflecting something of the nature of the new, and to some threatening, urban phenomenon. Nineteenth-century England was steadily developing into a nation which was losing its rural roots as cities and towns expanded. Victorian London, the largest city on the island of Britain, was a place where classes, voices, opinions and life-styles often clashed. It struck many observers as discordant, intractable and incomprehensible. For an artist like Dickens, however, London provided the raw material with which he could most happily and inventively work.

In the work of Dickens's contemporaries, such as Thackeray and Trollope, the metropolis remains largely incidental. Events take place in London because London in Thackeray and Trollope is a focus of fashionable, legal, political, cultural and commercial life. Their characters live, work, legislate and socialize in the city, or they visit it in order to transact business, but the city and its streets are often left unspecific. They are never so in Dickens's novels. Thackeray and Trollope tend to draw their characters from the upper strata of society, rarely moving their social perspectives downwards from the professional classes. Dickens, by contrast, selects characters from all walks of life. If anything, he seems to manifest a distaste for the upper classes which some of his more snobbish critics assumed was a consequence of his ignorance of them. Trollope's characters, in particular, tend to be the denizens of Parliament, or of aristocratic drawing-rooms, or of law-courts. Dickens's characters move from upstairs to down-stairs, from the salon to the slum, from the built-up West End to the straggly suburb. Few are leisured and those that work elbow their ways to work through thronged streets. Their work can vary from the legitimate to the nefarious, from pen-selling and pen-pushing to street-sweeping and street-walking. Dickens's London is a dense, varied and untidy place, but its people know how they and their city interact one with another. Not only do they know the difference between a villa in Norwood and a tenement in Soho, the nature of suburban Norwood and intensely urban Soho helps to define them. The fog which permeates the London streets in *Bleak House* is not just an unpleasant aspect of the city weather; it is elemental. It moulds consciousnesses and becomes an emblem of the very confusion that typifies the life of Victorian London.

Dickens's Victorian readers were well aware of how extensively and accurately he knew contemporary London. His friend, some-time collaborator and admirer George Augustus Sala, who once

Charles Dickens Museum

Dr Manette's House, off Soho Square, c. 1910. Dickens describes this house in *A Tale of Two Cities* as 'quiet lodgings … in a quiet street not far from Soho-square … the front windows commanded a pleasant little vista of street that had a congenial air of retirement on it'. Soho Square had been laid out in 1681 and it has long been assumed that Dickens housed Manette in part of what was known as Carlisle House, constructed *c.*1685 and a private hotel when Dickens wrote his novel. The house was destroyed by bombs in May 1940

described himself as 'of the streets, and streety', paid fulsome tribute to Dickens in an obituary notice.

> He was a great traveller … Where he had travelled longest, where he had looked deepest and learned most, was in inner London. He is no Regent Street lounger: he scarcely ever mentions Pall Mall; he rarely alludes to Piccadilly; he is not so much at home in fashionable squares; he is not to be found in the Ladies' Mile; he is out of his element at Brompton, or in the Regent's Park, or in Great Gaunt Street, or at Greenwich, or Richmond, or in any of the localities so well beloved by Thackeray. But he knew all about the back streets behind Holborn, the courts and alleys of the Borough, the shabby sidling streets of the remoter suburbs, the crooked little alleys of the City, the dank and oozy wharfs of the water-side. He was at home

in the lodging-houses, station-houses, cottages, hovels, Cheap Jacks' caravans, workhouses, prisons, school-rooms, chandlers' shops, back attics, barbers' shops, areas, back yards, dark entries, public-houses, rag-shops, police-courts, and markets in poor neighbourhoods.

As Sala also recognized, this very familiarity with the seamier side of life was the very stuff of Dickens's creativity:

Curiously, from these localities, unseemly and unsavoury as they might be, he brought pictures of life and manners, and produced characters of men and women and children that have been the wonder and delight and edification of millions, not only of his own countrymen, but of strangers at the uttermost ends of the earth.

Dickens had become, therefore, not simply the great explorer but also the great explicator.

Bedford Square, c. 1900. This is the finest Georgian Square in London, constructed in 1775–86 and still recognizable. Never at the extreme of fashion, it was inhabited in Dickens's day by prosperous professional people

The Quadrant, Regent Street, looking towards Piccadilly Circus, c. 1850. The colonnades, which formerly shaded the pavement and gave the Quadrant its particular elegance, were removed in 1848. They had been blamed with providing shelter to London's many prostitutes. The St James's Hall, where Dickens gave readings in 1861, 1866, 1868 and 1870, had an entrance here, though the main entrance stood round the corner in Piccadilly. The hall was demolished in 1905 and was replaced by the Piccadilly Hotel. The remaining buildings disappeared in the 1920s

It is with Sala's tribute in mind that we can best approach the fascinating thesis put forward by the Italian critic, Franco Moretti, in his *Atlas of the European Novel 1800–1900* (first published in Italian in 1997 and translated into English in 1998). Moretti uses maps to expound a highly original and flexible view of the nineteenth-century novel. His comments on the English tradition are particularly revealing. He pinpoints, for example, the diverse European settings of English Gothic fiction. He explores both Jane Austen's predominantly southern English locations and the colonial ramifications of her novels in comparison to those of Maria Edgeworth and Amelia Opie. When he approaches the work of Dickens, he readily recognizes the extent to which the novelist centres his fiction on London and he interestingly concentrates his observations on one early novel, *Oliver Twist*, and one late novel, *Our Mutual Friend*. His balance of an analysis of Balzac's Paris against one of Dickens's London is especially effective (though he admits that he generally prefers Balzac's work!). Moretti's contention is that Balzac's Paris is 'oriented by desire', it is a city shaped by 'daydreams … grand projects, erotic fantasies, imaginary revenges, sudden epiphanies'. In Balzac's hands it is a more varied and stimulating city than Dickens allows London to be and it is made exceptional not only by its great public spaces, its squares, its boulevards, its fashionable shops and its brightly lit palaces, or by the squalor of its poor inner suburbs, but by the existence in its very centre of the *rive gauche*, the socially mixed, unfashionable, arty, intellectual Latin Quarter. 'How much did British culture lose,' Moretti provocatively asks, 'by not having a Latin Quarter?' It is a speculation to which it is impossible to respond adequately.

Let idle speculations rest. Nevertheless, what Moretti is arguing is that the great cities of literature somehow need a kind of 'middle ground' between the purlieus of the rich and the slums of the poor, between aristocratic luxury and the shabby greyness of the masses. What he ideally wants is some raffish, stylish and classless Anglo-Saxon Bohemia. He might have uncovered the occasional morally unconventional household in Chelsea or Kensington, or even a loose gathering of artists' studios in Soho or Fitzrovia, but such free-thinking families were not commonplace. Certain of Dickens's friends and acquaintances managed to maintain deeply unconventional households (one only has to think of Wilkie Collins's open sexual *ménages* or of the 'marriage' of George Henry Lewes and George Eliot). But then neither Collins nor Lewes chose to live in districts (had they existed) where such relationships might have been winked at. There were plenty of ill-heated garrets, but hungry poets and impecunious painters who flaunted their misery were relatively uncommon in Victorian London, certainly when compared with what contemporary Paris had to offer. Nineteenth-century English artists and intellectuals were generally far too concerned with stylish respectability to bother with cultivating Bohemian tastes (one only has to recall the princely studio-houses built for themselves by Sir John Everett Millais and Lord Leighton). London's two university colleges, both established in the opening decades of the nineteenth century, were situated in the Strand and in Gower Street respectively, but it took nearly a century after the founding of University College before intellectuals began to gravitate to Bloomsbury. Apart from the Inns of Court, London had no historic centres of learning. London's 'middle ground' tended, therefore, to be identified with a middle class which was often indifferent to both art and the life of the intellect.

The fictional representation of Victorian London that Moretti explores is essentially one of stark contrasts. These contrasts are at times rather *too* stark. In commenting on pre-Dickensian urban fiction in England, for example, he identifies two fictional modes against which the young Dickens defined himself: the so-called 'Silver Fork' fiction centred on fashionable life in the West End of

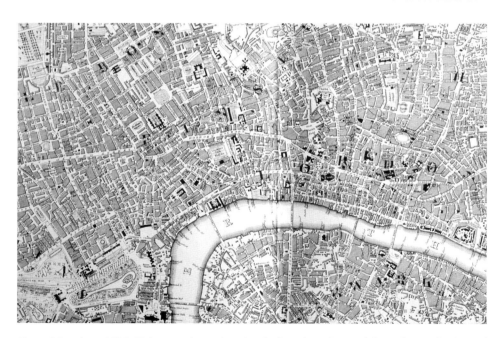

Central London, 1832. This map shows London before the advent of the railway. The line of Holborn and Oxford Street is broken at St Giles's and south of it lie Fleet Street and the Strand. There is a noticeable absence of north–south thoroughfares, however

London, and its polar opposite, the 'Newgate' novels which dealt with the criminal underclass. Both modes were popular with readers in the 1830s, and both used distinctive London settings, but neither, Moretti contends, showed a 'whole' city. He somewhat unjustly includes *Oliver Twist* amongst his 'Newgate' novels and argues, through a telling use of maps, the extent to which Dickens eschews reference to the West End in the novel. Dickens, we are told, shows Sikes and Oliver leaving on their night expedition to Chertsey. In describing their journey, Dickens allows us to follow their progress in great detail from the East End until they reach Holborn 'then the novel skips several miles, and starts again when they are well west of Hyde Park'. This, and the observation that *Oliver Twist* only focuses 'on one half of London', are valid enough. What Moretti fails to grasp, however, is that *Oliver Twist* does offer us a picture of a London which is not exclusively populated by the criminal classes. Unlike Balzac's representation of a socially and culturally diverse Paris, Dickens's vision of London is oriented on a predominantly *middle-class* response to the idea of 'desire'. Characters' ambitions, throughout Dickens's work, are directed not towards riches or aristocratic glamour, but towards financial security and bourgeois respectability. This is as true of *Oliver Twist* as it is of any of Dickens's later and more complex works of fiction. Time and again in Dickens's novels aristocratic pretension is exposed simply as that – pretension – while aspirations to easy wealth are seen as deceptive and even morally base. As *Great Expectations* pointedly suggests, the social values of the 'gentleman' are false unless they are combined with hard work, moral worth and respectability. These solid values distinguish the self-helping, and often self-made, middle classes both from the do-nothing luxury of life in the West End and from the misery and penury of the insalubrious alleys frequented by Fagin and Bill Sikes. The London of *Oliver Twist* may conspicuously lack a Latin Quarter, and Mr Brownlow's Clerkenwell is certainly no adequate substitute for it, but what Clerkenwell represents in the novel is Dickens's vital social and fictional middle ground.

Moretti seems to be somewhat more sympathetic to the significance of dull, middle-class London in his fine discussion of *Our*

Mutual Friend, but his sympathy is limited. He sees the novel as unifying 'the two halves of London' and as rendering the city a 'whole' and 'a single system'. He argues that in the long coach ride from the West End to Limehouse, taken early on in the novel by Mortimer Lightwood and Eugene Wrayburn, Dickens is conveying a new mastery of urban space and that this mastery is 'a stroke of genius'. For Moretti, *Our Mutual Friend* explores 'a third London … a sort of wedge, that holds the two extremes together'. This 'wedge' is formed by the centrally situated Temple, the legal enclave where Mortimer and Eugene 'receive visits from all parts of London'. Nevertheless, Moretti seems to be troubled by the repeated sugges-tion that in *Our Mutual Friend* his 'third London', an exclusively bourgeois London, has acquired 'an autonomous … *dominant* narra-tive role'. The London of the novel is, he tells us, 'quite simply, the world of the English middle class', a middle class that is 'surrounded by hostile forces'. In the fashionable West End there is 'fraudulent arrogance' while the docks to the east are the seat of 'physical violence'. To my mind he takes this idea of a beleaguered Dickensian middle class far too far:

> What is to be done then? Keep a distance from London is Dickens's reply: work in the City, and in the evening leave for the suburbs – like Nicholas Nickleby, John Carker, Wilfer, Harmon, Tom Pinch, Mr Morfin … a real historical trend clearly enough, but transmuted by Dickens into a symbolic paradigm which elevates the middle class above all other social groups (and in fact, above the social universe altogether) … At London's two extremes, in other words, *life and labor coincide*: social classification – *class* – is always unmistakeably present. But in the middle, the work/home dialectic allows Dickens's middle class have truly *two lives*: a public one in the work place – and a private one at home. A social existence, or perhaps a social 'mask' in the City, like Wemmick in *Great Expectations*: and then at Walworth, in the suburb, a home, a truer *moral existence*.

This is well observed, but it remains an exaggeration, even a distortion, of Dickens's method according to Marxist principles.

We should perhaps recall at this point that the founders of the Marxist project were London residents and that both spent their latter years in London suburbs (Karl Marx in Kentish Town and Friedrich Engels in the slightly more salubrious Primrose Hill). The very existence of the suburbs of London, both 'inner' and 'outer', did not automatically imply a split between work and home, between the private and the public. As much of the remainder of this study will show, Dickens was representing a real and recognizable London in his novels. He describes the suburbs not simply as retreats from snobbery and/or violence, but integral to the physical reality of London. To my mind, Moretti conveys the impression that the Victorian middle classes were somehow playing truant from their civic duties and that decisions about what we would now call life-style involved reneging on urban life. The city's suburbs were in fact where Victorian Londoners of all classes chose to live. Nineteenth-century London was emphatically not the contained urban space that Paris was. Parisians, for the most part, rejoiced in the pleasures and disadvantages of their distinctly urban space. Their contemporaries in London had both a more varied space and more choice as to how and where they lived. London sprawled, and Londoners increasingly, and contentedly, spread themselves over what had been, even in recent memory, a landscape of fields and farms and villages. Dickens represents the reality of London's urban spaces. Parisians thought of themselves as part of an entity; Londoners, on the other hand, were able to rejoice in variety.

Moretti's maps are both exemplary and revealing, but what they fail to explore is the fact that the English tended to hanker for a lost rural contentment far more than the French. When they cultivated their gardens those gardens could often be found close to the centre of the city. They often seem to have thought that the country need not be excluded from the city. Indeed, many held that the rustic and the urban could intermix in the ideal suburb, or, as the later Victorians described them, the 'garden suburbs'. This is where the urban landscape of the nineteenth century can properly be seen as 'political'. The French, with much justice, felt that the nineteenth century had been cut off from the eighteenth century by the Revolution of 1789 and by the Napoleonic Empire. Between the two centuries a great gulf was fixed and that gulf proved to be unbridgeable (despite the conservative efforts of the restored Bourbon kings and their successor regimes). The English middle classes did not contemplate a similar historical chasm. They, by contrast, seem to have hankered nostalgically for the old values and for a predominantly rural culture. The post-Romantic English were often inclined to sentimentalize the 'olden times' and a rural idyll that probably never existed. Nineteenth-century Paris and nineteenth-century Parisians had inherited a civilization which had been disrupted by political revolutions and aborted restorations, but their city continued to be the handsome urban focus of national life and the arbiter of a fractured culture. The English of the Victorian period had experienced no such political earthquake, but the changes wrought by economic and industrial change had proved equally disruptive. It had cut them off from a rural-based economy and severed links with the land. French governments, whether royal, revolutionary or imperial, had attempted to impose uniformity, and that uniformity helped to determine the architectural distinction of Paris. In Britain in the late 1820s and the early 1830s the governing classes had gradually accepted the principles of plurality and gradualism over the idea of radical reform. Representative, rather than autocratic, government was also central to British political self-definition.

The constitutional differences between France and Britain in the first half of the nineteenth century were reflected in the architectural, social and topographical natures of the capitals of the two countries. The city of Paris had clear boundaries (in the form of its customs wall – the *octroi* – and its *barrières*), and a clearly defined and centralized government. Victorian London, as we shall see, had no such borders and no such discipline. It was, to all intents and purposes, a series of administrative parishes which shared a vast urban space and often conflicted with one another's interests. The Paris Dickens knew was administered by a state official, the Prefect of the *département* of the Seine, and by a council of five members. The Prefect and his council were responsible for all public buildings and public works, for churches, streets, markets, hospitals, military institutions and even public fetes. The city was in turn subdivided into twelve *arrondissements*, each with its own elected mayor, though supreme authority rested with the Prefect of the Seine.

Dickens's London had its Lord Mayor and Corporation, of course, but this mayoral authority did not stretch beyond the historic confines of the City. The rest of London, sprawling to the west, north, south and east of the City, remained divided into once rural parishes (the names of St Martin's and St Giles's 'in the Fields' tell us how rural they once were). Some of these parishes were extensive, others tiny; some were rich, others desperately poor. Parisians probably felt that they *belonged* to the city of Paris and Paris to them. Victorian Londoners could be easily forgiven for feeling more loyalty to the parochial boards of St Marylebone or Stepney than they did to a Lord Mayor who was necessarily indifferent to their affairs. The unreformed governance of early Victorian London therefore reflected the fact that Britain had so conspicuously escaped the political cataclysm of the French Revolution and the centralizing zeal of Napoleon's administrative reforms. Britons in general might well have congratulated themselves on their distaste for imperial tyranny and revolutionary slate-wipings, but few would have considered the government of London a model for other nations to imitate.

What the Victorian British had not escaped, however, were the changes brought about by industrialization and by the stupendous growth of the national economy since the 1750s. Hand in hand with this economic growth had been a burgeoning of the population. For Londoners this meant a steady increase in its inhabitants of around 20 per cent per decade. By the mid-nineteenth century London had a population of over 2 million people (that is, seven times the size of Manchester, ten times that of Birmingham and approximately twice that of Paris). It is small wonder that this steady increase provoked ambiguous reactions. There was understandable pride in Britain's commercial achievement, but with it there came a sense of dismay at the social consequences of a rapid, unconstrained and seemingly unstoppable development. London was a phenomenon and a wonder of the world, but it was also a problematic phenomenon. As its prosperity and its population grew so did its slums. As the better off moved into more capacious houses, in newly constructed and cleaner and better-ventilated areas, the houses they abandoned were left to structural decline and to multi-occupation by the less well off. London's suburbia had begun to develop in the late seventeenth century. By the mid-nineteenth century inner city decay and the irregular and socially diverse suburbs were an inescapable fact of London's life.

Paris, as we have noted, was ringed by its customs wall, the *octroi*, first established in the 1780s. In the 1840s these walls stretched for some 26,000 yards and were crossed by fifty gates or *barrières* (although several of the most imposing gates survive to the present day, the *barrières* and their nightly closure are now perhaps most familiar from their appearance in the third act of Puccini's *La Bohème*). Carriages passing through the *barrières* were stopped and passengers' personal documents examined; commercial vehicles and carts were searched and duties were levied on all taxable articles. The monies collected from those bringing country produce and other goods into the city served as a kind of rate, dedicated both to charitable purposes and to the upkeep of the city. The old wall was extended outwards in 1860 to the line of Paris's considerable fortifications (thereby trebling the area contained within them). Thus the Paris Dickens knew was both contained and regulated in a way that was deeply unfamiliar, and would almost certainly have been uncongenial, to Londoners. In an important way, the country was excluded from Paris. London and Londoners, by contrast, steadily moved out into, and mingled with, the adjacent countryside.

Equally significantly, Victorian London had no outer ring of fortifications that served both for defence and to impose military order on those within and those approaching the city. When Victorian Londoners hankered for country air, they could move freely backwards and forwards at any time of the day and night. A law-abiding man like Dickens's David Copperfield, who settles with Dora in the suburban village of Highgate, can walk home unmolested after midnight, while a criminal like Bill Sikes can freely leave the city at night on his nefarious missions. Dickens's own nocturnal perambulations of London, to which we shall frequently return during the course of this study, were also only possible due to the unrestricted nature of the exits from, and approaches to, the metropolis.

Londoners of all classes lived in suburbs because the suburbs were affordable, reachable and unrestricted. An absence of planning laws generally allowed ambitious landowners to develop their estates in an unimpeded manner. They would do so with an eye both to the enhanced income to be derived from their property and to the tastes and pretensions of potential residents. Not all such developments worked as originally intended. The Somers Town estate to the north of Bloomsbury was, for example, leased to developers in the 1780s by the Somers family. The assumption was that a projected grand polygonal square containing thirty-two houses would attract well-to-do inhabitants. It was not to be. By the early 1800s the carcases of unfinished and unoccupied houses were sold for less than the value of the building materials and the area became the preserve of the lower-middle and working classes (including, briefly, the Dickenses). The area also attracted hard-up refugees (including many poor *émigrés* from Revolutionary France). By contrast, the development of the Grosvenor Estate in Belgravia, in the more fashionable west of London, from the 1820s to the 1850s turned an area of scrubby marshland into a stuccoed version of Mayfair.

Both Somers Town and Belgravia were essentially developments of squares and streets lined with terraced houses (some of which, in the case of Belgravia, aspired to be palaces). Both were essentially urban in style and intent. But when the Crown Estate, under the picturesque eye of the architect John Nash, proposed developing what would become Regent's Park in the 1810s and 1820s the original plans sought to evoke a far more rustic feel. Substantial villas surrounded by large landscaped gardens were part of the proposal from the beginning, but in the north-west corner of the estate two 'villages' of more modest detached houses (or 'cottages') were constructed. Built on the principle of what was called *rus in urbe* ('the country in the town'), these became the models on which subsequent London speculative developers worked. New 'villages', or 'village-style' developments, enjoyed a long-standing vogue amongst the middle classes. Surviving parallels can be seen further to the north-west along the Regent's Canal (in what is now known as Little Venice) and to the south of London in streets in Stockwell running off the Brixton Road (Dickens's newly married brother, Frederick, moved to what was described as a 'very charming & comfortable house' in 'a Swiss style' in Lorn Road, Stockwell, in 1848). The desire to find an alternative, anti-urban life-style on the outskirts of the city was increasingly the preserve of the more discriminating leaseholder. When the red-brick Bedford Park was developed at Turnham Green in the 1870s it rapidly took on the nature of an ideal colony for the artistically inclined, and consequently became the butt of contemporary satire about the pretensions of soulful aesthetes. Nineteenth-century Londoners, unlike their contemporary Parisians, could choose to inhabit 'villagey' suburbs which were populous variations on Marie-Antoinette's escapist *hameau* in the park at Versailles. The great difference lay in the fact that these suburbs were set not in parkland away from the city but at a convenient commuting distance from London. They were also communities and not the preserve of a privileged elite. As we shall see, other Londoners, most notably Mr Wemmick in *Great Expectations*, attempted to take this fantasy of rural escapism in the suburbs into the realm of cultivated eccentricity.

It cannot be overemphasized that the suburban London that we glimpse in Dickens's novels is not the exclusive preserve of either the well-to-do or the eccentric. Nor, as we shall see, are Dickens's commuters predominantly drawn from the prosperous middle classes. His walkers to work from the outer suburbs to central London include not only Wemmick from Walworth, but Bob Cratchit from Camden Town and Reginald Wilfer from Holloway. As a boy Dickens himself is said to have relished the very reverse of an 'escape' into suburbia. His biographer, John Forster, tells us that the novelist loved the sight of St Paul's 'looming through the smoke' when viewed from the family home at Bayham Street in suburban Camden Town. The looming dome seemed to represent the enchantment of what he saw as the 'real' London. As Forster describes it, the boy's greatest treat, however, was 'to be taken for a walk into the real town, especially if it were anywhere near Covent-garden or the Strand'. This would 'perfectly entrance him with pleasure'. In a memorable phrase Forster also records the young Dickens's 'profound attraction of repulsion' when he encountered the slums near St Giles's and Seven Dials, places where there were 'wild visions of prodigies of wickedness, want, and beggary'. It is small wonder, therefore, that the adult writer rejoiced in this concept of a London in which domesticity and beggary lived, if not quite cheek by jowl, certainly in a physical and geographical relationship to one another. The metropolitan core, the slum and the suburb, more than simply co-existed: they formed a creative symbiosis which profoundly stimulated Dickens's imagination.

Dickens's London was a city that proclaimed its confusing variety to its visitors and its inhabitants alike. It was not so much beautiful as compelling. It often confounded analysis. One particularly astute

A view of St Paul's from the River Thames, c. 1830. This steel engraving shows the increase in both the warehouses on the north bank of the river and the commercial traffic on barges

16 Bayham Street, Camden Town, *c.* 1900. This photograph shows the house where the Dickens family lived in 1823. It was demolished in 1910

critic of Dickens's Walter Bagehot, put his finger on why the nine-teenth-century city so appealed to the particular cast of the novelist's mind:

> It may be said that Mr Dickens's genius is especially suited to the delineation of city life. London is like a newspaper. Everything is there and everything is disconnected. There is every kind of person in some houses; but there is no more connection between the houses than between the neighbours in the lists of 'births, marriages, and deaths'. As we change from the broad leader to the squalid police-reports, we pass a corner and we are in a changed world. This is advantageous to Mr Dickens's genius. His memory is full of instances of old buildings and curious people, and he does not care to piece them together. On the contrary, each scene, to his mind, is a separate scene – each street a sepa-rate street. He has, too, the peculiar alertness of observation that

is observable in those who live by it. He describes London like a special correspondent for posterity.

Dickens had trained as a journalist, but he does not necessarily write like one. What Bagehot implies is that the novelist relished the disparities evident in contemporary London. These disparities were akin to those with which a Victorian newspaper presented its readers. The newspaper reader was not necessarily required to make sense of these self-evident inconsistencies, but Dickens the novelist felt an obligation to transform the disparate evidence of London into a coherent, even syncretic, form of fiction. As Bagehot suggests, it was in that very process of transformation that Dickens gave nine-teenth-century London a fresh relevance which serves to transcend the limitations of time. He made sense of the London he knew, and we latter-day readers interpret the nature of the Victorian metropolis through him.

If nineteenth-century London was hard to grasp in its entirety, and if its multifaceted, crowded streets confused most Victorian observers, the same could be said of the shape and format of most of Dickens's middle and late novels. Henry James famously (and rudely) described the standard form of the nineteenth-century novels as 'loose baggy monsters', but in Dickens's case these 'monsters' were capable of reflecting the nature of the London in which he set his fiction. While London may not have exactly been 'loose' or 'baggy', it was certainly sprawling, untidy and ill governed. Political and economic theory conspicuously failed to explain away its problems. Apart from wholesale reform, perhaps only fiction was sufficiently flexible and inventive to make some of those problems less perplexing. From first to last Dickens's fiction faced readers with London's seemingly intractable social problems, and from first to last that fiction offered some kind of resolution (albeit a fictional resolution). The twists and complications of his plots mirrored something of the tangle of the city's streets and of what Bagehot called the 'disconnections' of London life. To an important degree Dickens was also able to use the serial form in which he habitually published to explicate and unwind the complications of his plots. The process was gradual and the uncoverings, the unmaskings and the revelations came only as part of a drawn-out process. Monthly part serialization allowed Dickens to explore the inter-relationships of a multitude of characters over a period of some nineteen months.

Dickens had used monthly part serialization since the beginning of his career as a novelist, but his mature novels suggest an even greater relish for complex and interwoven lines of plot. Habituated readers of the 1850s and 1860s were almost certainly accustomed to Dickens's methods and to the fact that he would slowly unwind a series of destinies. This did not make his plots any easier to grasp and the opening chapters probably dismayed most new readers (to some extent they still do, especially when a novel like *Bleak House* is adapted for television). What readers had come to expect, however, was that Dickens would very gradually make clear that each of his multiple and often disparate characters would fit into a shapely and over-arching plot. Characters would, to an important degree, 'find their places'. The opening numbers of *Bleak House*, *Little Dorrit* and *Our Mutual Friend* must have challenged certain original and impatient readers. The first number of *Bleak House* of March 1852, for example, had two distinct narrators, a third-person narrator for the first two chapters and a first-person female narrator (Esther Summerson) who takes up what seems to be a tangential in chapters three and four. The third-person narrator sets the scene of a foggy London centred on a Chancery case. He then moves us abruptly to Sir Leicester and Lady Dedlock at their country house in Lincolnshire (where they are visited by the lawyer, Mr Tulkinghorn). Esther takes up a seemingly different story in Chapter 3, telling us of her lonely girlhood in Miss Barbary's household before gradually introducing us to a series of new characters: Richard Carstone, Ada Clare, Mr Guppy, Miss Flite and the Jellyby family. Having opened his novel with the single word 'London', Dickens's narrative seems to veer backwards and forwards from London. *Little Dorrit* may lack a double narrative, but it has a similarly disconcerting opening. The novel's first three chapters, which made up the first monthly part in December 1855, move us from a prison in the French port of Marseilles, to a party of travellers held in quarantine in the same port and, finally, to Arthur Clennam's

London Bridge, c. 1900. This early twentieth-century photograph shows the Bridge that Dickens knew. It was built in 1823–31 and opened in great state by King William IV in August 1831. We are looking northwards towards St Magnus the Martyr Church and the Monument. To their right is the Custom House of 1814–17. The photograph was taken by the steps on the south side of the River Thames where Nancy fatally reveals her secret to Rose Maylie and Mr Brownlow in *Oliver Twist*. The Bridge was demolished in the late 1960s and was incongruously rebuilt in the Arizona desert at Lake Havasu City

homecoming to 'gloomy, close and stale' London on a Sunday evening.

Both *Bleak House* and *Little Dorrit* are predominantly London-centred novels, but both move us to a focus on the city only gradually and unsteadily. Both novels may be said to open London up to a larger world, but both make us vividly aware of the confusions and disparities both of the city and of the characters who all necessarily gravitate to it. *Our Mutual Friend* is far more firmly centred on the metropolis as the long opening sentence, which forms its first paragraph, insists:

In these times of ours, though concerning the exact year there is no need to be precise, a boat of dirty and disreputable appearance, with two figures in it, floated on the Thames, between Southwark Bridge which is of iron, and London Bridge, which is of stone, as an autumn evening was closing in.

We open on the dreary river amongst the scavenging poor. Chapter 2 moves us abruptly upwards socially to the Veneerings' dinner party. They are 'bran-new' people, in a 'bran-new' house in a 'bran-new' quarter of London. They have money and pretensions, and their dinner guests reflect their upward mobility. It is at this dinner that readers first learn of the dysfunctional Harmon family, of the inheritance of dust, and of the disappearance of the family heir John Harmon. This information is imparted through the account given to the dinner party guests by Mortimer Lightwood. Chapter 3 expands on this story and then leads us back to the murky lower reaches of the River Thames when Charley Hexam conducts Mortimer and Eugene Wrayburn through London from the fashionable West End to the infinitely less savoury docks 'down by Ratcliffe, and by Rotherhithe.' This is, as Franco Moretti remarks, a journey which unifies 'the two halves of London' and sees London as 'a whole, as a single system'. But, significantly, this is not where the first number ended. The fourth chapter jerks us northwards again, to lower-middle-class Holloway and to the tensions within the Wilfer family.

The first monthly part of *Our Mutual Friend* therefore exposes a far more socially complex London than Moretti would have us believe. It is, none the less, a disconcerting London and a city full of dissociations. At the top we have the pretensions of the *nouveaux riches*; below them the indifferent involvement of Dickens's lawyers, Mortimer and Eugene; below that the family of a classically Dickensian clerk, and, at the bottom a sub-class of river scavengers represented by Gaffer Hexam and Rogue Riderhood. The novel will, of course, show us how each section of society is, in fact, closely inter-related, but that is certainly not obvious from the structure and social divisions of the four opening chapters. What Dickens is saying to his readers is that this is the nature of the London of 'these times of ours'.

Our Mutual Friend opens with both disparities and with a covert statement of the novel's evolving thematic structure. This structure only becomes obvious once readers advance through the evolving narrative. The scavengers and the Harmon dust-heaps with which we are presented in the opening chapters introduce us to the idea that the London of the novel is made up of a detritus of dissociated fragments, a rather less hygienic one than that suggested by Walter Bagehot. Bodies are lost and found, robbed and misidentified. Dust has been collected and heaped up; it is then sifted, graded and ultimately recycled. The heir to that dust disappears and is presumed to have been drowned in the River Thames. Inheritance and marriage plans are frustrated. In an important way the nineteenth-century idea of the recycling of urban waste material emerges as a key to our understanding of how the novel functions. Initially, dust and money are equated for both suggest a deathly corruption of the human spirit. But, on another level, the same dust-heaps stand for modern London as a whole. They are miscellaneous, random and an ultimate expression of a deathly redundancy. Yet, ironically, they have proved to be a source of immense wealth and they will prove to contain within them a key to regeneration. In no sense could *Our Mutual Friend* be seen as an early 'green' statement of the importance of waste recycling, but the novel does vividly remind us of the significance of finding new contexts and new uses. Gaffer Hexam and Rogue Riderhood make a living out of the human detritus they drag from the River Thames and in the first chapter of the novel Lizzie Hexam's father insists to her that not all the flotsam is mortal. He stresses that the river has been a source of 'meat and drink' to his family. But the disconnected fragments in the dust heaps and the essentially decontextualized corpses in the river both bear on the ideas of investigating associations and finding new contexts with which Dickens plays as his novel develops.

As the plot of *Our Mutual Friend* evolves, Dickens even extends the range of his play with the notion of recycling and the reassociation of fragments. When he was well advanced with the planning of his story the novelist introduced a new character: Mr Venus, the taxidermist and articulator of skeletons. According to Dickens's illustrator, Marcus Stone, he discovered the original of Venus's 'little dark greasy shop' at Seven Dials in the area of London that had fascinated him since his boyhood. The discovery of Venus's original, at Stone's prompting, was a brilliant instance of what is called serendipity, a combination of good fortune and an inspired instinct for the unusual.

> One evening in the early spring of 1863 ... [Dickens] told me he had a personage who had just appeared upon the scene who was to have some eccentric calling that would suit him. I had that same day been to see a certain Willis who lived in Seven Dials, who was an articulator of skeletons, a stuffer of birds, and dealer in bottled monsters. I suggested Mr Willis, or rather his occupation, as an idea that might be suggestive. 'It is the very thing I want,' he said, 'it couldn't be better.'

Marcus Stone would probably have sought out Willis's shop because it sold the kind of material that was useful to Victorian artists (who were trained to acknowledge the importance of human and animal anatomy). For Dickens, however, Venus was probably implicit before he became explicit as a character. His trade offers us a wry variation both on the central themes of the novel and on Dickens the novelist. Both are articulators, and both offer new associations to what had once seemed to be dissociated. Venus is intensely proud both of his trade and of his ability to give new meaning to the miscellaneous objects which are crowded into his shop. He explains the lay-out of his workshop and its contents to Silas Wegg.

> My working bench. My young man's bench. A Wice. Tools. Bones, warious. Skulls, warious. Preserved Indian baby. African ditto. Bottled preparations, warious. Everything within reach of your hand, in good preservation. The mouldy ones-a-top. What's in those hampers over them again, I don't quite remember. Say, human, warious. Cats. Articulated English baby. Dogs. Ducks. Glass eyes, warious. Mummied bird, Dried cuticle. Warious. Oh, dear me! That's the general panoramic view.

One object in the shop seems to elude Venus's manifest skill as an articulator. Despite the fact that he boasts to Wegg that he can sort out jumbled sack-loads of skeletons and can 'name the smallest bones blindfold equally with your largest' he admits that he has not yet found a proper use for the twisted bones of Wegg's amputated leg. These deformities, hidden in the recesses of Venus's shop, 'can't be got to fit in', even in one of his 'miscellaneous' skeletons made up of bones that can boast an international provenance. Nevertheless, Wegg's inconvenient and probably unusable leg-bones also serve Dickens's narrative purpose. They also, uncannily, parallel his authorial method. *Our Mutual Friend,* in common with all of Dickens's other London novels, offers an articulation of the city and, through fiction, attempts to make some shapely sense of it. But, given the very nature of Victorian London, not everything fits neatly and not everything can find a predesignated place even in the kind of novel that Dickens produced. Fiction merely reflects and interprets reality; it can neither photographically reproduce it nor offer a quasi-scientific analysis of it. True harmony is inevitably elusive, even in a novel partly centred on the dust-heaps of 'Harmony Jail'. The very nature of *Our Mutual Friend* accepts that the miscellaneous, the inconsistent and the stubbornly inconvenient co-exist with the 'tidyings up' that characterize Dickens's plots.

Of all the great Victorian novelists, Dickens is the most acute observer of London. He is also the most gifted transformer of incidental, and seemingly inconsequential, detail into the stuff of fictional consequence. The novelist described his method of observing London to a visiting American, G. D. Carrow, in 1867. Carrow had expressed a particular admiration for Dickens's 'descriptions of London', 'pictures' that the novelist himself claimed to have derived from personal observation.

When in the worst parts of the city my invariable precaution was to seem not to notice any person or thing in particular. I would walk along slowly, preserving an air of preoccupation, and affecting as nearly as possible the ways of a collector of house rents or of a physician going his rounds. When any scene of especial interest attracted my notice I usually halted at a crossing as if waiting for a conveyance or as if undecided which way to go. Or else I would stop and purchase some trifle, chatting with the vendor and taking my time for making a selection, or would order a glass of half-and-half, wait for the froth to subside, and then consume an hour in sipping it to the bottom. In my visits to the dens of thieves and other haunts of infamy, I deemed it prudent to associate myself with a brace of policemen who were well versed in the ways of the localities I wished to examine, and who introduced me to the professionals as an old friend who was making the accustomed round with them merely for the opportunity of a talk about old times. These were what I called my field-days. I suppose, sir, that I know London better that any one other man of all its millions.

Carrow's reporting of Dickens's voice may not have the truest ring of authenticity but the gist of what he records the novelist as saying does seem to offer a true picture of how he accumulated the details that make his fiction so very intense. Dickens was, as he himself emphasised to Carrow, a Londoner amongst Londoners, a Cockney in a Cockney world. He knew both the idiosyncrasies of Londoners and the sprawling and untidy city in which they lived. He knew London intimately both in its thronged public places and in its darkest and most arcane corners. What habitually attracted his notice was what most other observers probably eschewed because it appeared to be merely inconsequential or wretched or dangerous. What makes Dickens the novelist so remarkable is his very habit of observing and accruing fragments of city life coupled with an extraordinary facility in transforming them into the stuff of fiction. If Victorian London lives for us more vividly in the pages of Dickens's novels than it does anywhere else it is not just the result of a fortuitous coincidence of the hour and the man. Dickens is unique in that he possessed a singularly innovative genius. He also had a distinctive creativity that was sparked by the disconcerting and miscellaneous variety of modern urban living.

CHAPTER ONE

Dickens's Metropolis

'How do you like London?' Dickens's pompous Mr Podsnap enquires of a hapless foreign visitor in *Our Mutual Friend*. The nonplussed foreigner at first appears not to understand the question, so Mr Podsnap explains that he means 'London, Londres, London', and that the city must seem both very large and very rich to a foreign visitor. The visitor replies that it is indeed *énormément riche* only to be condescendingly told that his pronunciation is defective. Podsnap then tries a third conversational gambit, this time with leading words stressed by inferred capital letters: ' "And Do You Find, Sir," pursued Mr Podsnap, with dignity "Many Evidences that Strike You, of our British Constitution in the Streets Of The World's Metropolis, London, Londres, London?" ' The poor foreigner's command of the English language seems to collapse under the pressure of this assault, but Podsnap refuses to let the question of London's, and Britain's, greatness rest: 'We Englishmen are Very Proud of our Constitution' he loudly insists, 'It Was Bestowed Upon Us By Providence. No Other Country is so Favoured as This Country.'

Dickens approves neither of Mr Podsnap's pomposity nor of his arrogant nationalistic assumptions. Nevertheless, such assumptions were not uncommon among the more unimaginative of Podsnap's middle-class contemporaries. Take, for example, the journalist J. Ewing Ritchie's statements about the newly reconstructed Houses of Parliament in his book *Here and There in London* of 1859:

Not far from Westminster Abbey ... stands the gorgeous pile which Mr Barry has designed, and for which, in a pecuniary sense, a patient public has been rather handsomely bled. Few are there who have looked at that pile from the Bridge – or from the numerous steamers which throng the river – or loitered round it on a summer's eve, without feeling some little reverence for the spot haunted by noble memories and heroic shades – where to this day congregate the talent, the wealth, the learning, the wisdom of the land ... The House of Commons is a mixed assembly ... It is an assembly right in the main. Practically it consists of well-endowed, well-informed business men – men with little enthusiasm, but with plenty of common sense and with more than average intellect, integrity and wealth ... It boasts the brightest names in literature, in eloquence, and in law. Our island-mother has no more distinguished sons than those whose names we see figuring day by day in the division lists.

The Houses of Parliament, c. 1860. This photograph shows the masons' yards on the unembanked Thames and the barges used to transport materials for the construction of the building

Any reader of Dickens might readily suppose that the novelist would have choked reading those words. He would have profoundly disagreed with virtually every one of Ewing Ritchie's clauses except, perhaps, the one ruing the cost of Charles Barry's new Palace of Westminster. Dickens would have known the old palace well. As a junior shorthand reporter, he had recorded what passed for parliamentary oratory in the old House of Commons a building which had been reduced to a burnt-out shell in the fire of 1834. This early experience of recording the workings of Parliament gave him a lifelong distaste for the institution and a pervasive scepticism concerning its honourable members. 'My faith in the people governing,' Dickens famously told an audience in September 1869, 'is, on the whole, infinitessimal; my faith in The People governed is, on the whole, illimitable.'

Dickens's decidedly low view of 'the people governing' was not uncommon. It was, for example, eloquently reiterated in the work of his mentor and friend, Thomas Carlyle. Nevertheless, relatively few amongst their Victorian contemporaries failed to be impressed by the building that housed parliament. A guidebook to London of 1850 told its readers that the Palace of Westminster was 'one of the most magnificent buildings ever erected continuously in Europe' and concluded that it was 'probably the largest Gothic edifice in the world'. One distinguished anti-democrat, the surprisingly fanciful Tsar Nicholas I of Russia, is even said to have described the unfinished new building as 'un rêve en pierre' – a dream in stone. For many British voters the Houses of Parliament not only represented the finest achievement of modern architecture; they also seemed to embody the antique glory of the British Constitution, a glory which had been renewed by the reforms of the 1830s. The tall clock-tower, and the chimes of Big Ben, the great booming bell it contains, rapidly became identified not just with a burgeoning democracy but also with the very spirit of London.

Despite this, it should not strike readers of Dickens as strange that the novelist should so rarely deign to mention either the Palace or the resonant chimes from its clock-tower. When Dickens crosses Westminster Bridge at night in the essay 'Night Walks', for example, he is grudgingly prepared to admit that 'the external walls of the

British Parliament' are 'the perfection of a stupendous institution ... and the admiration of all surrounding nations and succeeding ages' but he feels obliged to add that the institution is 'perhaps a little the better now and then for being pricked up to its work'. Dickens was not unresponsive to the Palace's architecture, but he could not rid himself of the suspicion that its outward splendour merely offered a shelter to the widespread humbuggery and windbaggery inside. It may seem ironic therefore that his mortal remains should rest in Poets Corner in Westminster Abbey, not only in the shadow of the Houses of Parliament but also in a spot in the Abbey where, during the quieter hours of the day, the chimes of Big Ben echo so clearly.

In Time and Out of Time

It may well be that Dickens so rarely mentions the new Palace of Westminster because the old jumble of historic buildings that made up the old palace loomed larger both in his memory and in his imagination. Certainly in *Bleak House*, a novel in which the slow workings of parliament and the law are so steadily criticized, the Court of Chancery is seen sitting both at Lincoln's Inn and in Westminster Hall. If, as we are led to suppose, the novel is set in a period before the passing of the Reform Act in 1832, Westminster Hall must still have been hemmed in by old buildings, not all of which were to survive the fire of 1834. *Bleak House* is not unique in terms of its historical setting. Dickens's non-historical fiction appears to be set in the period of the novelist's boyhood and early manhood. This is when he first got to know London intimately. The two historical novels (*Barnaby Rudge* and *A Tale of Two Cities*) are exceptions, of course, but *Pickwick Papers* is specifically dated to the late 1820s and *Little Dorrit* to the mid-1820s. Most of the other novels have the London of the early 1830s as their setting. Much of the action of *Oliver Twist* of 1837–9 takes place in contemporary London, while *Our Mutual Friend*, 1864–5, opens with reference to 'these times of ours'.

Depending on their social status, most of Dickens's Londoners and visitors to London move to and from the city by stagecoach, chaise or carrier's cart. Within the city, they walk or they take horse cabs. The advent of the railway, and the extraordinary changes brought about by railway travel, is either a new phenomenon (as in *Dombey and Son*) or one that remains to be realized. Slightly old-fashioned business premises, Scrooge's or the offices of the Cheeryble brothers for example, are still located in the City of London, but the City is also where the likes of Mr Dombey conducts his business. Scrooge still lives in the City, as does the decidedly decrepit Mrs Clennam in her even more decrepit house, but Mr Dombey is one of many businessmen who have chosen to live in the West End. By the time of Dickens's death in 1870 the City of London was virtually depopulated. This depopulation was the result of social and economic changes, very rarely of the kind of sensational structural collapse that befalls the creaking Clennam house.

The desperately poor in Dickens's novels live in slums which had either been demolished or redeveloped by the 1870s. Much of the notorious St Giles rookery was knocked down when New

Charles Dickens Museum

Jacob's Island, c. 1840. This engraving shows the notorious Thames-side slum described in *Oliver Twist*. The river's tides and the streams that fed into it made Jacob's Island a breeding-ground for cholera

Dockhead, Jacob Street, Jacob's Island, Bermondsey, *c.* 1890. Reputedly the site of Bill Sikes's demise in *Oliver Twist*. This evocative view suggests something of the once notoriously run-down area of Jacob's Island. All the buildings in this photograph have disappeared

Oxford Street was cut through it as early as 1847, though there was sufficient human misery remaining in the area for Dickens to describe it in the essay 'On Duty with Inspector Field' of 1850. In the same year, the novelist was insistent that the cholera-infested Jacob's Island, where Bill Sikes dies in *Oliver Twist*, truly existed but in the 1867 edition of the novel he was constrained to admit that it was 'much improved and changed'. As Dickens wryly noted in 'On Duty with Inspector Field', however, few people seemed to ask 'where the wretches whom we clear out, crowd'. The wretches, it seems, moved on, taking slum-land with them. Often they would colonize areas of the inner city which had once been the preserve of the better off. The middle-class suburbs of the 1830s, in what is now thought of as 'inner London', have tended to enjoy a far better record of survival, but throughout Dickens's lifetime London's stock of bourgeois terraces and suburban villas was being steadily amplified. New developments offered more salubrious residences further

46

from the smoky heart of the city. Victorian readers of Dickens would readily have recognized the city he described as emphatically the London they lived in, yet those same readers knew that Dickens's London was a place of change and development. Once in a while, in the face of what often appeared to be official indifference, that change was dynamic.

The Governing and the Governed

One of Dickens's most consistent complaints relates to the lack of a proper response to London's problems by both national and local government. He was to insist in his essay 'On Duty with Inspector Field' that Londoners had consistently been offered placebos rather than positive action:

> With such scenes at our doors, with all the plagues of Egypt tied up with bits of cobweb in kennels so near our homes, we timorously make our Nuisance Bills and Boards of Health, nonentities, and think to keep away the Wolves of Crime and Filth, by our electioneering ducking to little vestry-men, and our gentlemanly handling of Red Tape.

Similar complaints echo throughout *Bleak House*, a novel in which Dickens's fictional slum, Tom-all-Alone's, festers and breeds its dangerous diseases while politicians merely debate remedies. In Dickens's time the City of London, under its Lord Mayor and Corporation, was regarded as an efficient enough system of local government – so much so that in 1837 the Municipal Corporations Commission reported that it was the only local administration in the kingdom that did not need reform. Dickens, who had no love for lord mayors and their sumptuous annual banquets or for the aldermen who served under them, might not have agreed with this benign assessment. The City had, however, only a very limited jurisdiction when it came to the administration of the sprawl of London. The City Corporation, rich and powerful as it was, only controlled what is loosely called 'the Square Mile' north of the

River Thames and three parishes in Southwark south of the River (known as 'Bridge Ward Without'). It guarded both its privileges and its boundaries jealously.

The rest of London was either administered or, as the case may be, maladministered, parish by parish. Parishes, meeting in a vestry, elected churchwardens (their number varying from parish to parish) and paid for a vestry clerk, generally a professional lawyer. This creaking, unrepresentative, antiquated and inefficient form of local government was classically what we would now call 'Dickensian'. In one of his 'Sketches' of 1835 the young novelist had satirized the election of a beadle, the local official charged with collecting the poor rate and keeping order in the streets. In 1852 he returned to the pomposity and petty-mindedness of a London parish election in the essay 'Our Vestry'.

> To get into this Vestry in the eminent capacity of Vestryman, gigantic efforts are made, and Herculean exertions used. It is made manifest to the dullest capacity at every election, that if we reject Snozzle we are done for, and if we fail to bring in Blunderbooze at the top of the poll, we are unworthy of the dearest rights of Britons. Flaming placards are rife on all the dead walls in the borough, public-houses hang out banners, hackney-cabs burst into full-grown flowers of type, and everybody is, or should be, in a paroxysm of anxiety.

To further damn the process of election and the deliberations of the elected vestry Dickens even resorts to one of his most considered insults: 'Our Vestry is eminently parliamentary. Playing at Parliament is its favourite game.' Thus the parish merely serves to extend ineptitude downwards from the state to the street corner, from a Prime Minister to a Bumble, from Westminster to Tom-all-Alone's.

Many of the London parishes were overwhelmed by the kind of social problems that local vestries were inadequately equipped to tackle. Some were compact and rich, others straggling and desperately poor. Nor was poverty confined to the East End. Yet others, including those in the inner West End, such as St Anne's, Soho, and St Margaret's, Westminster, intermixed areas of relative prosperity with those mired in dire poverty. Only in 1855 was a Metropolitan Board of Works established by central government. It was the first metropolitan-wide authority, with a jurisdiction over what was later to become the County of London. Ancient parishes were not abolished, but old vestries, which had formed the ancient basis of London's local government, were reconstituted. Each was given the power to choose, depending on size, either one or two members of the 45-member Board. These members were not directly elected, and parishes which retained sufficient clout managed to delay or avert the imposition of a truly efficient system of local government. Nevertheless, the Metropolitan Board of Works did oversee the construction of London's Victorian sewerage system (1865–75) and, related to it, the Victoria Embankment of the north side of the Thames (1864–70) and the Albert Embankment to the south (1866–70). These great works

Charles Dickens Museum

The Victoria Embankment, c. 1900. The construction of the Embankment, completed in 1870, alleviated not only problems in traffic circulation but was also related to London's improved drainage and sewage systems. It radically diminished the muddy expanses once exposed at low tide

were planned and executed by the Board's Chief Engineer, Joseph Bazalgette, but they were only realized in the last years of Dickens's life and are therefore barely touched on in his writings. A London County Council, superseding the Metropolitan Board of Works, was created in 1888 but local vestries survived until the London Government Act of 1899. The City of London remained outside the jurisdiction of both the Metropolitan Board of Works and the London County Council (though it lost Bridge Ward Without, its only residential suburbs south of the river). It still fiercely maintains its independence from the rest of the capital, thus rendering London something of an anomaly among the great cities in the world.

The census of 1841 revealed that there were over 270,000 houses in London, many of which stood over a cesspit. In poor areas these cesspits had a distressing tendency to seep up through the floorboards of the houses above. When, in 1847, a Metropolitan Commission on Sewers insisted that the use of cesspits should be discontinued the result was that most of London's human waste went into one of the 369 sewers, most of which discharged ordure directly into the River Thames. The Thames, being a tidal river, was supposed to flush itself twice a day, but polluted with the waste material of some 3 million inhabitants, it did so sluggishly and inefficiently. It was also distinctly malodorous. In the exceptionally hot and dry summer of 1858 the stench from the river was so great that the windows of the Palace of Westminster had to be draped in curtains saturated in chloride of lime in an attempt to kill the smell. Londoners had to endure a summer that was known thereafter as the Season of the Great Stink. Benjamin Disraeli, never lost for colourful words, was led to describe the river as 'a Stygian pool reeking with ineffable and unbearable horror'.

The Thames as it appears in Dickens's novels is the noxious and heavily polluted river that predated Bazalgette's innovatory drainage systems. The somewhat less rank river of the 1830s supports the jolly jaunts described in Sketches by 'Boz' ('The River' and 'The Steam Excursion' for example) and in Chapter 40 of Martin Chuzzlewit Tom Pinch and his sister Ruth take a happy stroll 'down among the steam-boats on a bright morning' and rejoice

Rotherhithe, *c.* 1890. The working Thames as Dickens would have known it, though there are already improvements in riverside housing evident to the left

in the 'tiers upon tiers of vessels' on the Thames. Nevertheless, in *Our Mutual Friend*, 1864–5, the murky river figures more systematically and dramatically than in any other of Dickens's novels. By now it, and the poor who live on its banks on its lower reaches, seem to share in the state of vitiation and contamination: 'Down by Ratcliff, and by Rotherhithe; down by where accumulated scum of humanity seemed to be washed from higher grounds, like so much moral sewage, and to be pausing until its own weight forced it over the bank and sunk it into the river.' The Thames, which provided the grandest entrance to London and its port from the sea, had, by the mid-nineteenth century, also become its shame.

Echoing Footsteps

The London that the young Charles Dickens first got to know in the 1820s was crowded, unhygienic and generally ill governed. Its pattern of streets was tangled and disorganized, its buildings were blackened and its atmosphere was dank and polluted with the smoke of hundreds of thousands of domestic coal fires. With some notable exceptions, little seemed to change during the novelist's thirty-odd years as the most popular and influential writer in England. The introduction of the Metropolitan Police Force during Sir Robert Peel's tenure as Home Secretary in 1829 had given the city a vastly improved system of law enforcement, but the very success of the new police made the general public more aware of the pervasive problems of crime and poverty in the capital. Dickens, a consistent admirer of the police, and in particular of the Detective Department of the force, made it clear in his novels and essays that a good policeman was familiar with those parts of the metropolis that few respectable citizens dared venture into. Dickens's night-time adventures with one particularly distinguished senior police officer are vividly described in the essay 'On Duty with Inspector Field' but it is the intrepid Inspector Bucket in *Bleak House* who best embodies what the novelist saw as most admirable in a vigilant London policeman. In Chapter 22 of the novel Bucket leads Mr Snagsby into the dirty maze of Tom-all-Alone's, shining his bull's-eye lantern as he proceeds.

> When they come at last to Tom-all-Alone's, Mr Bucket stops for a moment at the corner, and takes a lighted bull's-eye from the constable on duty there, who then accompanies him with his own particular bull's-eye at his waist. Between his two conductors, Mr Snagsby passes along the middle of a villainous street, undrained, unventilated, deep in black mud and corrupt water – though the roads are dry elsewhere – and reeking with such smells and sights that he, who has lived in London all his life, can scarce believe his senses. Branching from this street and its heaps of ruins, are other streets and courts so infamous that Mr Snagsby sickens in body and mind, and feels as if he were going, every moment deeper down, into the infernal gulf.

Like Bucket's bull's-eye lantern the enterprise of the Metropolitan Police had exposed London's dire social problems to public scrutiny.

It had also heightened the debate about the causes and effects of London's problems.

Virtually everyone agreed that London was big and that it was growing bigger by the decade. Its size was the most significant element in what was seen as its unmanageability. Foreign visitors to London from the early 1800s onwards were often dazzled by its sheer magnitude, and they were equally shocked at its dirt, its milling population and its haphazard confusion. Native observers were somewhat more sanguine. Many of those native commentators, and particularly the writers of guidebooks, were genuinely proud that London was the greatest city in Europe and the most populous on Earth. The authors of Tegg and Castleman's *New Picture of London for 1803–4, or A Guide through the Immense Metropolis* were happy to give facts and figures, though they seem to struggle with them:

> London is of such an irregular form that it is difficult to ascertain its extent; its length from east to west is above seven miles; its breadth in some parts is above three; in others two; and in others, little more than a mile and a half. It contains nearly 8000 streets, lanes and alleys, and about 160,000 houses, warehouses etc. It was supposed to contain a million of inhabitants, but its population does not exceed 840,000; the air is extremely salubrious; the principal streets are broad and well-paved, and are in general kept remarkably clean.

This sounds as if everything is dandy and largely unproblematic. Nevertheless, with an increased fascination with statistics and with the advent of decennial censuses from 1841 a more accurate picture of the real size of the population of London began to emerge. By 1811, the year before Dickens's birth, the city was believed to contain some 1,139,355 inhabitants. There was an additional 300,000 by 1831 and in 1841 the figure had reached 1,949,277. This, one commentator observed, was double that of the entire population of England and Wales at the time of the Norman Conquest. During the next three decades the population continued to explode. In 1851 it had reached 2,363,341, in 1861 it was 2,808,494 and in 1871 it was 3,261,494. These are the figures for what we would now call 'Inner London'. They do not include the population of outer suburbia and the further-flung semi-rural villages of Kent, Surrey, Middlesex and Essex which are an essential part of London. By contrast, the population of Paris within the *barrières* (which defined its extent) was estimated to be a mere 909,126 in 1836. This rose to the more substantial 1,106,891 when that of the *département* of the Seine was included. At the time of Dickens's death in 1871 Greater Paris contained 1,851,792 people while the population of Greater London and its outer suburbs had risen to 3,840,595.

In 1854 Bohn's *Pictorial Handbook of London*, a volume originally produced for visitors to the Great Exhibition of 1851, could happily proclaim in its opening paragraph:

> London is the largest and wealthiest, as well as the most populous of the cities of the world. It is at once the centre of liberty, the seat of a great imperial government, and the metropolis of that great race whose industry and practical application of the arts of peace are felt in every clime, while they exert an almost boundless influence over the moral and political destinies of the world.

This is imperial self-confidence of the first order, a self-confidence worthy of Dickens's Mr Podsnap, but it does not really tell us much about London. Bohn's *Handbook* does, however, go on to provide its readers with highly informed sections concerned with London's hydrography, its climate, its geology and its natural history, before giving us a surfeit of the kind of human statistics of which the Victorians were so fond. There were, for example, 18,246 marriages, 58,362 births and 18,246 deaths recorded in the capital in 1841. In the same year there were some 278,093 houses of which 11,324 were uninhabited. Ten years later the number of houses was believed to be above 300,000 situated in some 10,000 streets and alleys. Amongst its working inhabitants London had 6,450 butchers, 9,110 bakers and 3,591 brass workers (who probably count as candlestick makers). Amongst the professions most commonly described by Dickens there were 20,932 clerks, 39,300 male servants, 138,917 female servants and nurses, 19,240 public servants (including 6,000 policemen), 2,399 lawyers, 27,049 dress-makers and seamstresses, 8,389 merchants, pawnbrokers and auctioneers and 50,279 labourers.

When it came to the condition of the unemployed and the unemployable, Bohn's *Handbook* describes the 'ample' provision of parish workhouses, ragged schools, hospitals and of benevolent establishments who variously aided the aged, the blind, the insane, the 'idiot', the would-be emigrant and the distressed needlewoman. Perhaps the most chilling section advises users of the *Handbook* on how to tackle the problem of London's indigent and persistent beggars:

> The Irish, from preference are clad in tatters, and walk barefoot; the smaller number of English beggars array themselves expressly for their performance, and if they have not some deformity

The Obelisk, St George's Circus, *c.* 1835. The Gothic-style Blind Asylum, or School for the Indigent Blind, opened here in 1831 and was demolish in 1901 when the school moved to Leatherhead. Beyond the school we can glimpse the Bethlehem Hospital (now the Imperial War Museum). As a boy, and the son of a debtor, Dickens had the value of his clothes 'appraised' 'at a house somewhere beyond the Obelisk' and he later passes this way in his memorable essay 'Night Walks'

assume it. They likewise hire infant children at considerable expense ... To every beggar, however urgent his appeal, and whatever guarantee he may offer of its truth, the stranger must thoroughly shut his ears and his pockets. If he is in doubt lest he should turn away any case of real distress, let him subscribe to the Mendicity Society in Red Lion Square, who will supply him with tickets to be given as relief instead of money, and who give food only to those who are found to be deserving. The beggars have been known and seen to give these Mendicity tickets to the really poor. The police, too, can be called upon to take charge of a beggar, and to see him on his way to the poorhouse or the House of Correction.

Visitors to London had, therefore, been forewarned: mendacity was not to be mistaken for mendicity.

The *Handbook* did not deny that there was 'a large amount of suffering in London', or that sometimes 'the victims of sensuality drop in their career of dissipation', or that the working population subjected itself 'to great privations to keep out of the workhouse'. A perusal of Dickens's novels might well have provided similar evidence, for Bohn's instances of suffering can be variously paralleled by the cases of Em'ly and Martha in *David Copperfield*, of Jo in *Bleak House* and of Betty Higden in *Our Mutual Friend*. Nevertheless, Bohn's *Handbook* was insistent that cases of 'utter wretchedness, and even death from want of food', were not to be taken as instances 'by which to measure the condition of the population'. The problems of poverty and indigence which so beset nineteenth-century London were not unique to London. Any reader of the novels of Balzac or Hugo or Dostoevsky will recognize that they also troubled those far more regimented cities of Paris and St Petersburg.

As Dickens was at pains to suggest, his British contemporaries dealt with poverty and the attendant problem of criminality either with indifference or with a ruthlessness that could readily be mistaken for heartlessness. Union workhouses, Benthamite model prisons, houses of correction and even the hulks, the mastless ship prisons which were moored near the Woolwich

Dockyard, offered what seemed like a proper deterrent to indigence and crime. As we have seen, when slum-clearance took place little official thought seems to have been given to where the displaced poor ought to attempt to rehouse themselves. For the most part, the redevelopment of slums and the construction of new thoroughfares through areas of social deprivation were taken as indications of progress. Unsurprisingly, visitors to London were not recommended to seek out prisons and workhouses or the dank courts and yards off the Mile End Road or the twisted lanes and alleys of St Giles's. London's poor were evident enough in the day-lit main streets of the capital; it was firmly believed that their night-time haunts were more properly the object of police surveillance rather than that of amateur curiosity. It is singularly unlikely that any twenty-first-century guidebook to a teeming megalopolis in the developing world would offer any different advice to tourists.

The Real and the Un-real City

Where the picture of London given in a Victorian guidebook differs from the vividly imaginative representation in Dickens's novels is essentially a matter of emphasis. A guidebook will select sights and sounds and views while offering a general survey of a given city; it will point out major monuments and recommend particularly colourful districts or points of vantage. Dickens, by contrast, takes London whole and, moreover, he takes it for granted. He fits his characters to places; he particularizes, not generalizes. Dickens the novelist is no cicerone guiding his readers on sight-seeing tours through the highways and by-ways of the city. The traditional 'sights' of London are largely incidental to Dickens's plots. He left it to his contemporary and sometime friend, William Harrison Ainsworth, to make the Tower or St Paul's or St James's Palace the focus of highly charged and fanciful romances. Thus, for Dickens, a 'dreary room' in the Tower of London merely serves as a prison for Lord George Gordon in *Barnaby Rudge* and the Tower itself is a 'sight' David Copperfield will take Betsey Trotwood to see during a visit to the capital. The bulk of St Paul's impresses the Yorkshire farmer, John Browdie, in *Nicholas Nickleby*, while its 'great black dome' helps Pip to orient himself when he explores London for the first time in *Great Expectations*. The cross on the summit on the dome is an object of puzzlement to Jo in *Bleak House* as he sits in a 'baking stony corner' of Blackfriars Bridge 'munching and gnawing ... until ... he is stirred up and told to "move on"'. Most memorably, perhaps, Peggotty expresses her grave disappointment on being taken to see the view from the top of St Paul's in *David Copperfield* because she remains more attached to the picture of the cathedral which had once adorned the lid of her work-box than she is to the building itself.

St Paul's, *c.* 1860. Stereoscope photograph taken from the corner of Paternoster Row

Walcot Square, Kennington Road, c. 1900. This triangular 'square' of 1837–9 survives intact. In *Bleak House* it is here that Mr Guppy leases 'a commodious tenement', a 'six roomer'

This is not to imply that Dickens is indifferent to London's monuments. It is just that he knows that monuments in themselves are very rarely indicative of a character's attitudes, habits or attitude to life. Ordinary London addresses, when Dickens's characters boast of them, tell us infinitely more. When we learn, for example, that Mr Pickwick lodges in a front pair of rooms in Goswell Street, and that the street life that he observes from his windows shapes his world view, it gives a key to Pickwick's character and social class but it does not really tell us much about the somewhat characterless Goswell Street. Another Islington address suggests a great deal about the brash law clerk, William Guppy. When Guppy ineptly declares his love for Esther Summerson in Chapter 9 of *Bleak House* he is explicit about the salubriousness of his and his mother's residences. Mrs Guppy lives 'in an independent though unassuming manner' in the Old Street Road; her son has 'an abode in lodgings at Penton Place, Pentonville', lodgings which are 'lowly, but airy, open at the back and considered one of the 'ealthiest outlets'.

59

When Guppy renews his proposal in Chapter 64 his financial and professional circumstances appear to have improved, though his low level of social sophistication appears to be constant:

'I *have* some connexion,' pursued Mr Guppy, 'and it lays in the direction of Walcot Square, Lambeth. I have therefore taken a house in that locality, which, in the opinion of my friends, is a hollow bargain (taxes ridiculous, and use of fixtures included in the rent) and intend setting up professionally for myself there, forthwith....'

'It's a six roomer, exclusive of kitchens,' said Mr Guppy, 'and in the opinion of my friends, a commodious tenement. When I mention my friends, I refer principally to my friend Jobling ... My friend Jobling will render me his assistance in the capacity of clerk, and will live in the 'ouse ... My mother will likewise live in the 'ouse, when her present quarter in Old Street Road shall have ceased and expired and consequently there will be no want of society. My friend Jobling is naturally aristocratic by taste; and besides being acquainted with the movements of the upper circles, fully backs me in the intentions I am now developing ... I wish to prove to Miss Summerson that I can rise to a heighth, of which perhaps she hardly thought me capable ... I beg to lay the 'ouse in Walcot Square, the business, and myself , before Miss Summerson.'

This is stomach-churningly embarrassing, and Dickens has caught Guppy, his pretensions and his tone of voice exactly. Dickens has 'placed' him precisely. Unsurprisingly, Esther feels able to reject Guppy for the second time. Like Penton Place in Islington, Walcot Square, which still survives intact off the Kennington Road, is a real place. It is an awkwardly shaped space, more a triangle of small terraced brick houses than a square in the proper sense of the term. It was constructed in 1837–9 and would therefore have been newly built when Guppy made his proposal. Guppy may be a man on the make, but his address in quintessentially petit bourgeois Walcot Square suggests that he still has a long way to go.

Three Churches

Dickens's use of certain London churches is also closely linked to the responses they evoke in his characters. The novelist was not particularly sensitive to the niceties of architectural style, but he was certainly alert to the way London's churches determine the nature of the areas in which they stand. Many modern readers might find his unresponsiveness to the baroque delights of Thomas Archer's St John's, Smith Square, Westminster, disconcerting. The church and the once seedy streets around it figure in *Our Mutual Friend*:

> Bradley Headstone and Charley Hexam duly got to the Surrey side of Westminster Bridge, and crossed the bridge, and made along the Middlesex shore towards Millbank. In this region are a certain little street, called Church Street, and a certain little blind square, called Smith Square, in the centre of which last

Charles Dickens Museum

Smith Square, Westminster, *c.* 1900. This is the 'blind little square' described by Dickens in *Our Mutual Friend*

retreat is a very hideous church, with four towers at the four corners, generally resembling some petrified monster, frightful and gigantic, on its back with its legs in the air.

Attitudes to English baroque architecture have shifted considerably since the 1860s and we should not necessarily expect Dickens to be sympathetic to the whimsy of Archer's idiosyncratic church. It once stood, hemmed in by early eighteenth-century houses, in an irregular square, the chief entrance to which from Millbank was Church Street (now Dean Stanley Street). Horseferry Road was a narrow by-way and there was no Lambeth Bridge. The square was effectively a quiet and seedy backwater and it was 'blind' because the streets that now open up regular views of the church post-date Dickens's time. His association of the building with something monstrous may strike us as strange, but it is probably related to the fact that Jenny Wren, the crippled dolls' dressmaker, lives in its

Charles Dickens Museum

St John's, Smith Square, Westminster, c. 1900. This photograph shows Thomas Archer's idiosyncratic church which Dickens seems to have found 'hideous'. We can see here the doors to the crypt through which Jenny Wren imagines thrusting local children and blowing pepper after them

shadow. Her corner house has 'a kind of deadly repose on it, more as though it had taken laudanum than fallen into a natural rest'. Jenny insists that the unnatural quiet of the street is disturbed by children 'screeching' as they play in the gutter or call through her key-hole and make fun of her physical deformity. For Jenny the 'hideous' church suggests a sadistic solution to her discomfort: 'There's doors under the church in the Square – black doors leading into black vaults. Well! I'd open one of those doors, and I'd cram 'em all in, and then I'd lock the door and through the key hole I'd blow in pepper.'

St John's still stands in the middle of Smith Square, though following damage in the Second World War it has been cleaned and refitted and now serves as a concert hall. It is difficult to recognize that the building could ever have appeared sinister. The vaults underneath are now a well-lit public restaurant and the only pepper dust likely to rise in the air there would be the result of an unfortunate culinary accident. It need scarcely be added that the now sought-after early-eighteenth-century streets around St John's contain some of the most expensive houses in London.

The church of St George-the-Martyr in the Borough is a far less inventive expression of eighteenth-century taste than St John's, Smith Square. It was built between 1734 and 1736 to replace a medieval church and it is prominently sited at the southern head of Borough High Street. Dickens would have known both the church and the chimes of its clock from the period of his unhappy boyhood when his father was imprisoned in the Marshalsea and he had lodgings in the somewhat drab Lant Street. 'There is a repose about Lant Street ... which sheds a gentle melancholy upon the soul' Dickens tells us in Chapter 32 of *Pickwick Papers*, doubtless reflecting on his own unhappy time there. Bob Sawyer, the appropriately named medical student at the nearby Guy's Hospital in *Pickwick Papers*, also lodges there and holds a party in his lodgings. Bob uses the church to indicate where his rooms are. ('Lant Street, Borough; it's near Guy's ... Little distance after you've passed St George's Church.') Drab the street remains, but the repose and the melancholy are now dissipated.

Charles Dickens Museum

Vestry, St George-the-Martyr, Borough High Street, *c*. 1900. This shows the now vanished vestry containing the parish registers. Here Amy Dorrit and Maggy spent the night, having been locked out of the Marshalsea, in *Little Dorrit*

The significance of St George's church for readers of Dickens, however, depends not on Bob Sawyer but on Amy Dorrit, 'Little Dorrit'. Amy, born in the Marshalsea, is baptized at the font in St George's with the turnkey standing as her godfather and returning to the prison 'like a good 'un'. At the opening of Chapter 9 of *Little Dorrit* the south-west wind roars through the church's steeple before it beats 'the Southwark smoke into the jail' and in Chapter 14, after spending too long at her 'party' at Arthur Clennam's, Amy and Maggy are obliged to spend the night in the church's vestry, having been locked out of the prison at closing time. The verger or sexton recognizes Amy as 'one of our curiosities' and proudly shows her the entry in the parish registers concerning her birth and christening, before making her up a bed of church kneelers with the burials register as her pillow. At the very end of the novel the 'child of the Marshalsea' returns to the church to be married as the light from a stained glass window of Christ the Saviour falls on her and Arthur. With the ceremony over, husband and wife 'walked out of the church alone':

> They paused for a moment on the steps of the portico, looking at the fresh perspective of the street in the autumn morning sun's bright rays, and then went down.
>
> Went down into a modest life of usefulness and happiness … They went quietly down into the roaring streets, inseparable and blessed; and as they passed along in sunshine and in shade, the noisy and the eager, and the arrogant and the forward and the vain, fretted, and chafed, and made their usual uproar.

This is perhaps the most haunting ending of any Dickens novel.

St George's, which has the distinction of appearing in two of Phiz's illustrations to the novel, has survived the vagaries of demolition, bombing and redundancy largely intact (though its stained glass eastern window, like the Marshalsea, is long gone). The church's stone steeple, the roaring of the London streets in front of it and the vain, fretful, chafing passers-by are, however, instantly familiar.

A third church, Marylebone Parish Church, is not mentioned by name in *Dombey and Son*, but is almost certainly where Little Paul Dombey is christened in Chapter 5 of the novel. Again, Dickens would have known this particular church well, for he had leased 1 Devonshire Terrace at the northern end of Marylebone High Street at the end of 1839 and had begun to plan the novel in the house before he left for Switzerland in May 1846. Mr Dombey, Dickens's City merchant, would have been a near neighbour. Dombey has a large house 'on the shady side of a tall, dark, dreadfully genteel street in the region between Portland Place and Bryanston Square'. This house would technically have lain in the parish of All Souls, Langham Place (built by John Nash 1822–4), but it is far more likely that Dickens was thinking of the more substantial structure which stands prominently in the Marylebone Road, then known as the New Road.

St Mary's, which was built in 1813–17 by the architect Thomas Hardwick, replaced an earlier medieval parish church, the interior of which had figured in a scene in Hogarth's *The Rake's Progress*. The new church, which has a prominent western steeple with a clock in the first stage, also has a churchyard to its side and, unlike All Souls, is shaded by trees. It is now approached through a dignified six-columned portico, flanked by two further columns on each side, but the original entry was via a circular vestibule on the north side. It was its now altered interior that evidently struck Dickens as appropriate to the gloomy Dombey christening. This interior, which was radically altered in 1883, once sported two tiers of galleries, a high mahogany pulpit and, opposite it, a mahogany reading desk. There was a further gallery, containing seats for charity children, above the altar. A large organ case occupied the east wall while the marble font stood under the northern gallery. It was a fine example of the Anglican style at its most respectably Protestant and its most stately neo-Classical.

This is how Dickens describes Little Paul's bone-chilling christening ceremony:

St Marylebone Parish Church, *c.* 1900. The church was built in 1813–17 and is almost certainly the church in which the Dombey family worship in *Dombey and Son*

'Please to bring the child in quick out of the air there,' whispered the beadle, holding open the inner door of the church.

Little Paul might have asked with Hamlet 'into my grave?' so chill and earthy was the place. The tall shrouded pulpit and reading desk; the dreary perspective of empty pews stretching away under the galleries and empty benches mounting to the roof and lost in the shadow of the great grim organ; the dusty matting and the cold stone slabs; the grisly free-seats in the aisles; and the damp corner by the bell-rope, where the black tressels used for funerals were stowed away, along with some shovels and baskets, and a coil or two of rope; the strange, unusual, uncomfortable smell, and the cadaverous light; were all in unison. It was a cold and dismal scene.

When the christening party arrives they have to wait for an equally 'dismal' wedding to finish. The union being forged is between a bride who is too old and a bridegroom who is too young and is therefore a distinct echo of the marriage in Hogarth's *The Rake's Progress*. Nevertheless, it is neither baptism nor marriage which seems to determine the nature of Dickens's response to the church: the funereal dominates, appropriately so given that this was where Paul's mother's obsequies had been performed only weeks before. Paul 'rends the air with his cries' as he is baptized.

Readers will already have guessed that the poor child has more of death about him than of life. Indeed, in Chapter 18, it will be in one of the vaults in the church that Paul's coffin will be deposited next to 'the perishable substance' of his mother. It will also be here that his father will plan to place a memorial tablet to his 'beloved and only child' (though Mr Dombey, who has a surviving daughter, has to be reminded that the inscription should read 'beloved and only *son*'). This same church will host Mr Dombey's second marriage in Chapter 31, though it does so with a bleakness worthy of that unpropitious event.

Dawn, with its passionless blank face, steals shiveringly to the church beneath which lies the dust of little Paul and his mother, and looks in at the windows. It is cold and dark … The steeple-clock, perched up above the houses, emerging from beneath another of the countless ripples in the tide of time that regularly roll and break on the eternal shore, is greyly visible, like a stone beacon ...

Hovering feebly round the church, and looking in, dawn moans and weeps for its short reign, and its tears trickle on the window-glass and the trees against the church-wall, bow their heads, and wring their many hands in sympathy. Night, growing pale before it, gradually fades out of the church, but lingers in the vaults below, and sits upon the coffins. And now comes bright day, burnishing the steeple-clock, and reddening the spire, and drying up the tears of dawn, following the night, and chasing it from its last refuge, shrinks into the vaults itself and hides, with a frightened face, among the dead, until night returns, refreshed, to drive it out.

This is Dickens at his most imaginatively poetic. Nothing in this description seems to offer the bride and groom, both of whom are widowed, much hope of unhaunted wedded bliss. Significantly

York Gate, Regent's Park, looking towards St Marylebone Church, 1827. Thomas H. Shepherd's engraving shows the newly completed church on the New Road (now Marylebone Road) closing the vista from Regent's Park. This is almost certainly the church in which Little Paul is buried in *Dombey and Son*

enough, when Florence Dombey and Walter Gay marry in Chapter 57, they pause on their way to their own wedding to look at 'a tablet on the wall' in this gloomy building, but the marriage ceremony takes place in a dusty but infinitely less daunting church in the City of London.

What Survives of Dickens's London?

St Marylebone Parish Church had been rebuilt on a new site to serve a singularly prosperous parish, one which had vastly expanded in the early years of the nineteenth century. The streets between Portland Place and Bryanston Square, where Mr Dombey lives, formed part of the Portman estate. Both Bryanston Square and the neighbouring Montagu Square were completed in about 1821 and were proclaimed by Thomas Smith's *Topographical and Historical Account of the Parish of St Mary-le-Bone* (1833) to be the 'best examples of well constructed town residences'. Residents included two retired admirals, the MP for Middlesex, the Austrian Ambassador and the French Consul-General. The houses were large, uniform and thoroughly respectable, though they might not have aspired to the very highest fashion. North of the church stretched Regent's (formerly Marylebone) Park, the fringes of which were laid out on Crown land by John Nash and Decimus Burton as a series of grand stucco terraces between 1822 and 1827. One of these grand terraces, York Terrace, was described by Thomas Smith in 1833 as a 'splendid row of princely mansions' which had 'the appearance of one single building rather than a row of private dwellings'. Engravings of these new terraces were given pride of place in Thomas H. Shepherd's *Metropolitan Improvements, or London in the Nineteenth Century* of 1827. Lavish praise was heaped on Nash's flamboyant designs for the great line of streets that led from Waterloo Place via the new Regent Street to the park in Shepherd's accompanying text, for, as he was at pains to point out: 'No city in Europe [had] undergone such rapid changes and improvements as this metropolis.' Although Regent Street was redeveloped in the 1920s nearly all of Nash's work

Charles Dickens Museum

Mr Dombey's House, *c.* 1900. This mansion in Bryanston Square was once associated with the house occupied by Mr Dombey who lived 'on the shady side of a tall, dark, dreadfully genteel street ... It was a corner house ... It was a house of dismal state, with a circular back to it, containing a whole suit of drawing rooms looking upon a gravelled yard, where two gaunt trees, with blackened trunks and branches, rattled rather than rustled, their leaves were so smoke-dried'

around the park has survived intact, as have the far plainer, brick-built western stretches of the Portman estate. Dickens, who rented a house at 3 Hanover Terrace in 1861, would readily recognize both areas.

It is notable, however, that, apart from Mr Dombey, the Podnaps (who have a house in Portman Square in *Our Mutual Friend*) and the Merdles (who live in Harley Street in *Little Dorrit*), relatively few of Dickens's major characters can afford such expensive accommodation. When Esther Summerson and Mr Jarndyce look for rented accommodation in *Bleak House* they select a 'cheerful lodging' over an upholsterer's shop near Oxford Street. One decidedly unfashionable denizen of the area north of Oxford Street, the one-legged ballad seller, Silas Wegg in *Our Mutual Friend*, does not actually live there at all, but sets up his stall outside a corner house 'not far from Cavendish Square'. Here he keeps his remaining foot warm by sheltering it in a basket in cold weather.

Many of Dickens's contemporaries had cold feet about the aristocratic West End in quite another sense. Those schooled by John Ruskin to admire the architecture of Venice considered the genteel squares and the straight, uniform, stock-brick streets in the area to be the quintessence of dullness. In his poem 'In Memoriam' of 1850 Tennyson somewhat jadedly characterizes Harley Street as 'long' and 'unlovely'. Dickens describes the Merdles' grand house in Harley Street as representative both of the architectural milieu of the area and of the pretensions of the rich and conservative upper middle classes who reside there. Both the houses and their residents possess a tiresome uniformity.

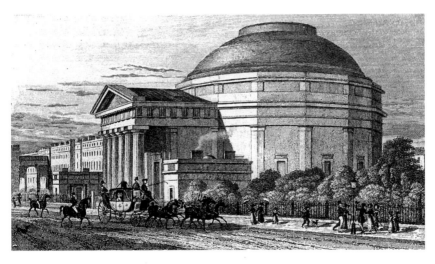

The Colosseum, Cambridge Gate, Regent's Park, 1827. Engraving by Thomas H. Shepherd. Built 1824–7 to house a panorama of London and finally opened in January 1829. Its name was a reference to its size rather than any resemblance it might have borne to the great Roman amphitheatre. The original enterprise failed and in 1831 the building was purchased by Dickens's friend, the tenor John Braham, in order to provide London with a multi-purpose entertainment space. Braham added two 'marine caverns' and an 'African glen' full of stuffed animals, and concerts were given in the evenings. It later became a Museum of Sculpture, with a Swiss chalet and mock classical ruins in its grounds. It finally closed in 1863 and was demolished in 1875

Hanover Terrace, Regents Park, seen from the Park, c. 1860. The terrace was designed in 1822 by John Nash. Dickens was a regular visitor to the house of Wilkie Collins's widowed mother here. The terrace survives

Like unexceptional Society, the opposing rows of houses in Harley Street were very grim with one another. Indeed, the mansions and their inhabitants were so much alike in that respect, that the people were often to be found drawn up on opposite sides of dinner-tables, in the shade of their own loftiness, staring at the other side of the way with the dullness of the houses.

Everybody knows how like the street, the two dinner-rows of people who take their stand by the street will be. The expressionless uniform twenty houses, all to be knocked at and rung at in the same form, all approachable by the same dull steps, all

Portman Square, Marylebone, c. 1900. This handsome Georgian square was laid out in the second half of the eighteenth century. Most of it has been ruined during the course of the twentieth century. It is where the Podsnaps live in *Our Mutual Friend*

fended off by the same pattern of railing, all with the same impracticable fire-escapes, the same inconvenient fixtures in their heads, and everything without exception to be taken at a high valuation – who has not dined with these?

Few modern readers will have had to endure such a boring and formal a dinner party as that offered by the Merdles. As most of Harley Street now house private medical practices and clinics even fewer modern readers are likely to have been bidden to dine there. Many a former dining room functions as a consulting room and several stately drawing rooms now serve as an operating theatre. Much of the street has been reconstructed both to conform to later canons of West End architectural taste and to provide appropriate professional accommodation. Few Victorians loved residential streets like Harley Street and even fewer would regret the addition of the red brick bays and fanciful stone flourishes which have relieved the old repetitive uniformity.

Charles Dickens Museum

Harley Street, *c.* 1900. This is the 'long, unlovely street' described in Tennyson's *In Memoriam*. It is the kind of straight, late Georgian street, lined with uniform houses, that many Victorians found boring. Harley Street was, nevertheless, a highly desirable residential area where the social pretensions of the Merdle family seem to be satisfied

Dickens seems to have had scant regard for the architecture of the even more fashionable Georgian streets south of Oxford Street. In the nineteenth century, before the arrival of the foreign embassies, hotels, apartment blocks and discreet but lavish casinos that now characterize the district, a select residence in Mayfair set the seal on many a pretension to high society. Dickens, who referred to the 'aristocratic gravity of Grosvenor Square' in *Nicholas Nickleby*, was well aware of its social *cachet*. At the very end of the eighteenth century the square's grand residents had included two dukes, one marquis, five earls and a bevy of noble widows. There was little evident thinning of the blue blood of mid-nineteenth-century residents. In Dickens's time the philanthropic 7th Earl of Shaftesbury lived for some thirty years at number 24 and the novelist's aristocratic friend, Edward Bulwer Lytton, spent the last five years of his life at number 12. In *Dombey and Son* Mrs Skewton borrows a house in Brook Street 'from a stately relative, who was out of town'. Despite her reduced circumstances, Brook Street seems to endow her with the requisite air of gentility for her to satisfactorily marry off her daughter, Edith, to the socially inferior Mr Dombey. Grosvenor Square retains its generous dimensions (nearly 6 acres) but hardly any surviving building in the square itself would be recognizable to Dickens's contemporaries. The Victorian aristocracy has long departed and their houses have been replaced by the intrusive twentieth-century bulk of the US Embassy and, on the other sides of the square, by neo-Georgian pomposity.

The area around Grosvenor Square does, however, retain a good deal of pre-twentieth-century architecture, some of it distinguished. Dickens's most extended series of references to Mayfair occur in *Little Dorrit*. When he has come into his considerable inheritance Mr Dorrit chooses to live in a hotel in Brook Street and there he is honoured with a call from the financier, Mr Merdle. Mr Tite Barnacle of the Circumlocution Office attempts to cling to 'aristocratic gravity' in an airless but expensive house in Mews Street, Grosvenor Square ('not absolutely Grosvenor Square itself, but it was very near it'). Whichever 'Mews Street' Dickens had in mind has long since disappeared during the wholesale redevelopments around the square. When Arthur Clennam visits Mr Barnacle he arrives at 'a squeezed house, with a ramshackle bowed front, little dingy windows and a little dark area like a damp waistcoat pocket'. Later in the novel Arthur and Mr Meagles return to Mayfair in search of Miss Wade who has taken a house in a 'parasite street' off one of the grander thoroughfares. Typically, the doleful Miss Wade has selected a residence in a 'long, regular, dull and gloomy' street, one that reminds the narrator of 'a brick and mortar funeral'. Dickens's generally jaded account of the area immediately to the east of Park Lane, however, still retains a certain validity:

They rode to the top of Oxford Street, and, there alighting, dived in among the great streets of melancholy stateliness, and the little streets that try to be as stately and succeed in being more melancholy, of which there is a labyrinth near Park Lane. Wildernesses of corner-houses with barbarous old porticoes and appurtenances; horrors that came into existence under some wrong-headed person in some wrong-headed time, still demanding the blind admiration of all ensuing generations and determined to do so until they tumbled down … Parasite little tenements with the cramp in their whole frame, from the dwarf hall-door on the giant model of His Grace's in the Square, to the squeezed window of the boudoir commanding the dunghills in the Mews, made the evening doleful. Ricketty dwellings of undoubted fashion, but of a capacity to hold nothing comfortable except a dismal smell, looked like the last result of the great mansions' breeding in-and-in; and, where their little supplementary bows and balconies were supported on thin iron columns, seemed to be scrofulously resting upon crutches … Here and there was a retiring public-house which did not require to be supported on the shoulders of the people, and where gentlemen out of livery were not much wanted.

This is clearly not the London that makes Dickens feel at ease. Everything seems to be designed to express pretension rather than comfort. This part of the West End shows off, but has in fact little to be proud of. His distaste seems to have been as much social as it was architectural.

Newly developed but singularly prosperous districts of Regency and early Victorian London, such as Belgravia, have only the most marginal existence in Dickens's novels. The narrator of *Our Mutual Friend* tells us that Lady Tippins 'dwells over a staymaker's in the Belgravian Borders', but that is virtually all we hear of this highly fashionable district. In *Nicholas Nickleby* the whimsically pretentious Mrs Wititterly has a house in Cadogan Place, 'the slight bond' that joins 'the aristocratic pavements of Belgrave Square' and the 'barbarism' of the still far from desirable Chelsea:

It is in Sloane Street, but not of it. The people in Cadogan Place look down upon Sloane Street and think Brompton low. They affect fashion too, and wonder where the New Road is. Not that they claim to be on precisely the same footing as the high folks of Belgrave Square and Grosvenor Place, but that they stand with reference to them, rather in the light of those illegitimate children of the great who are content to boast of their connections, although their connections disavow them.

'Barbaric' Chelsea was for the most part far too straggling a suburb to figure prominently in Dickens's novels, though it was very gradually establishing itself as an area hospitable to residents with an intellectual bent. Thomas Carlyle, whom Dickens regularly visited, had established his residence in Cheyne Row in 1834, largely because he had sought out an old house which was both economical to rent and distant from the hubbub which characterized more centrally placed districts. On taking the house, Carlyle insisted to his wife that the area was 'unfashionable', an aspect of Chelsea that only began to shift in the latter half of the century when both Rossetti and George Eliot took houses in Cheyne Walk.

Another area now readily associated with London's intelligentsia, Bloomsbury, had a very different social make-up in Dickens's day. The Dukes of Bedford had begun to develop their Bloomsbury estate in the late seventeenth century, but their investment in residential property was at its most expansive and profitable in the last years of the eighteenth century and in the first third of the nineteenth. Their mark was not only architectural; each new street and square bore a name somehow connected with the Russell family. Russell Square was begun in about 1800, Torrington Square dates from 1821–4, Tavistock Square from 1824 and Woburn Square from 1829. Thereafter developments northwards petered out until the 1850s. Thackeray astutely selected Russell Square as the residence of the Sedley family in *Vanity Fair*, clearly indicating that from the beginning Bloomsbury was rich and respectable rather than elegant and fashionable. The Sedleys would probably have been quite at home here with other newly prosperous merchants and professionals. As the blue plaques that seem to proliferate in the area clearly show us, central Bloomsbury's Victorian residents were substantially drawn from the professional classes, including eminent architects, surgeons, physicians, lawyers and men of learning. Any aristocratic presence is confined to a statue of

Francis, the seventh Duke of Bedford, who stares blankly down Montague Place.

As a consequence of the somewhat haphazard development of the northern part of the Bloomsbury estate a large plot on the east side of Tavistock Square was given over in the 1820s to the construction of three large brick houses separated from the square and from Upper Woburn Place by iron railings, a garden and trees. One of these houses, the eighteen-roomed Tavistock House, was bought by Dickens in October 1851. He stayed here for some nine productive years before moving himself and his family to Gad's Hill Place in Kent. Dickens, who, according to John Forster, seems to have had 'no particular sentiment of locality and any special regard for houses he had lived in', would probably not have minded that this particular London house was demolished in the opening years of the twentieth century. It and its neighbours were replaced by a building which has since become the British Medical Association. The novelist would still find most of the leafy Bloomsbury squares

Endsleigh Street, Bloomsbury, c. 1900. This street was laid out in the 1830s on the fringes of the Duke of Bedford's estate. Much of the estate survives, though the gates, which once ensured a certain degree of respectable privacy for residents, are long gone

Torrington Square, Bloomsbury, c. 1900. This lovely narrow square, lined with uniform terraces, was laid out in 1821–5. Christina Rossetti lived and died at No. 30. Her house survives but the majority of the Square was wrecked by the University of London in the 1970s

Charles Dickens Museum

familiar to him, but men and women who are familiar with Dickens's life are likely to regret that this memorable house, and the rooms that hosted his amateur theatricals in the 1850s, survive only as a memory (though the site of Tavistock House is now marked by one of Bloomsbury's most poignant blue plaques).

Dickens had begun married life in rented chambers in Furnivals Inn in Holborn but in March 1836 he and his wife, Catherine, moved to 48 Doughty Street. They were to stay here until November 1839. This late-eighteenth-century house is the only surviving major residence of Dickens in London and, having been acquired by the Dickens Fellowship in June 1925, it is now the Dickens Museum. When it was acquired it had long ceased to be occupied by one family and had done worthy service as a boarding house. This was the fate of many houses in the area east of

Tavistock House, Tavistock Square, Bloomsbury, *c.* 1890. The house to the right of the photograph was the one leased by Dickens in 1851–60. Here he completed *Bleak House, Little Dorrit* and *A Tale of Two Cities.* Here too he hosted his celebrated amateur theatricals. The house was demolished in 1900

Southampton Row, and it was one from which even the grander houses in Bloomsbury proper were not immune (Virginia Woolf and her siblings originally rented in the area in the 1910s because the houses were commodious but cheap). The streets stretching north from Doughty Street towards King's Cross Station are still full of modestly priced hotels though Doughty Street has resumed an air of professional respectability. Even when Dickens moved here in 1836 the somewhat undistinguished area to the east of Southampton Row already possessed an air of slightly shabby gentility, though Doughty Street itself was a private, gated road with a porter on duty at each end. The area also contained a good number of well-maintained lodging houses.

In two sketches entitled 'The Boarding House' which he published in *The Monthly Magazine* in 1834, Dickens described Mrs Tibbs's establishment in nearby Great Coram Street.

John Ruskin's birthplace, 54 Hunter Street, Bloomsbury, c. 1900. Ruskin vividly describes this house in his *Praeterita*. It is typical of a prosperous middle-class house of the early nineteenth century, many of which were sub-divided as lodgings (Mrs Lirriper's house in Great Coram Street was round the corner). All of these houses were demolished when the Brunswick Centre was built in the early 1970s

Charles Dickens Museum

The house of Mrs Tibbs was, decidedly, the neatest in all Great Coram Street. The area and the area-steps, and the street door and the street-door steps, and the brass handle, and the door plate, and the knocker, and the fan-light, were all as clean and bright as indefatigable white-washing, and hearth-stoning, and scrubbing and rubbing, could make them. The wonder was that the brass door-plate, with the interesting inscription 'MRS TIBBS,' had never caught fire from constant friction, so perseveringly was it polished. There were meat-safe looking blinds, in the parlour window, blue and gold curtains in the drawing-room, and spring-roller blind, as Mrs Tibbs was wont in the pride of her heart to boast, 'all the way up.'

This is a lost London of hearth-stoned doorsteps, polished brass and assertively moral domesticity, but the Dickensian lineage that stems

from Mrs Tibbs lives on in a succession of memorable urban land-
ladies from Mrs Bardell through Mrs Crupp to Mrs Lirriper. In 'The
Boarding House' sketches Dickens discovered not only a 'type' but
also his true *métier* as a London writer.

To the north and east of the Gray's Inn Road the parishes of
Clerkenwell and Islington had been extensively developed as residential suburbs in the first third of the nineteenth century. The
population of Clerkenwell more than doubled between 1801 and
1831 while that of Islington rose from some 15,000 in 1811 to
56,000 in 1841. The architectural reasons for this explosion in population can still be readily appreciated, for the area has been relatively
little redeveloped since the mid-nineteenth century and long
stretches of Georgian brick terrace and square remain intact. George
Cruikshank, who so tellingly illustrated Dickens's *Sketches by 'Boz'*
and *Oliver Twist*, had settled into a house at 25 Myddleton Terrace,
Pentonville (now Amwell Street) in 1824. Here he had a well-lit
studio on the top floor. It was the rapid development of Islington to
the north of his house that inspired his satirical etching entitled
'London going out of Town – or – the March of Bricks and Mortar'.
This etching of 1829 shows the City of London to the left, with St
Paul's and the Monument rising above the choking, domestic
smoke, while a forlorn signpost points to still rural Hampstead on
the right. Already skimpily built brick terraces, called 'New Street',
have been erected and there are 'To Let' signs appended to their
scaffolding. Beyond them a kiln literally belches out bricks into
fields from which haystacks and cows flee in terror. An advancing
army of chimney-pots forces one leafless tree to exclaim, 'I must
leave the field', while another trunk expires with the punning words
'Oh! I am mortarly wounded'. The leading chimney-pot, with a head
made out of a hod, carries a placard inscribed: 'This Ground to be
Let on a building lease: Enquire of Mr Goth, Brickmaker, Bricklayers
Arms, Brick Lane, Brixton.'

The new-built, sometimes gimcrack, bricky Islington would
steadily creep northwards to cover the erstwhile fields of Holloway
and the lower reaches of Highgate. One notable Dickensian
resident of Holloway, Reginald Wilfer in *Our Mutual Friend*, is
perhaps exemplary of Islington's predominantly lower-middle-class

LONDON going out of Town. or ‒ The March of Bricks & Mortar.' ‒

'London Going out of Town' or 'The March of Bricks and Mortar'. George Cruikshank's satirical etching of 1829 perhaps reflects the sprawl of London in the Islington area. It vividly evokes the rapid increase in suburban development in the first third of the nineteenth century

population. In one of his youthful *Sketches by 'Boz'* Dickens had described the 'early clerk population of ... Islington and Pentonville ... fast directing their steps towards Chancery Lane and the Inns of Court'. Neither the speculative builders of Islington nor the men and women who leased the houses they built ever really aspired to Belgravian elegance. 'It ought to be a cheap neighbourhood ... and not too far from London,' insists Tom Pinch in *Martin Chuzzlewit* when he proposes that he and his sister, Ruth, look for lodgings in Islington. They end up in 'a singular little old-fashioned house, up a blind street' where they rent 'two small bedrooms and a triangular parlour, which promised to suit them well'. It is in Islington too that Mrs Lirriper, Dickens's most doughty lodging-house keeper, originally sets herself up in business after the untimely death of her husband. Islington evidently proves an insufficiently salubrious neighbourhood, for Mrs Lirriper tells us that she soon transferred her establishment to the far less out-of-the-way 81 Norfolk Street, Strand, 'situated mid way between the

City and St James's', where she feels able to charge her prospective lodgers no less than 18 shillings a week.

The Coming of the Railway

Mrs Lirriper tells us in her narrative of 1863 that she advertises her lodging house in *Bradshaw's Railway Guide*. The mention of such an advertisement was far more than a sign of the times. It would have seemed to be a standard way of drawing attention to furnished lodgings in central London in the 1860s, for anyone travelling to London, on business or for pleasure, would have consulted their *Bradshaw*. George Bradshaw had first published what became *Bradshaw's Monthly Railway Guide* in 1839, and it rapidly became not only the standard work of reference for finding one's way across a by now national railway network but also a handy way of looking up

The Railway Dragon

'The Railway Dragon'. This satirical etching by George Cruikshank shows the disruptive nightmares associated with the arrival of the railways and suggests that the new technology was not always welcome. It was published in Cruikshank's *Table Book* in 1845

The Bull and Mouth Inn, St Martin's-le-Grand, 1817. This watercolour by George Shepherd shows this long-established City coaching inn, which served Manchester and Scotland. It was rebuilt in 1828 as the *Queen's Hotel*, though its new title was dismissed by one London guide book as 'very foolishly so-called'. It survived the advent of the railways as a City hotel with a distinctive, and often Mancunian, clientele. It was finally demolished in 1887 when the General Post Office expanded its premises

the times of local and suburban trains. It was not always totally reliable, as Dickens's highly amusing essay 'A Narrative of Extraordinary Suffering' (published in his journal *Household Words* in July 1851) serves to suggest. Nevertheless, both *Bradshaw* and the new phenomenon of the railway made an indelible mark on the British consciousness.

Mrs Lirriper's advertisement suggests something of the vast shift in perceptions of time, speed and mobility that had taken place in Britain since the 1830s. In *Pickwick Papers* (which is set in the 1820s) the Pickwick Club travels around England on stagecoaches and in *Nicholas Nickleby*, Nicholas, Squeers and the hapless prospective pupils at Dotheboys Hall use the same means of transport to reach the cold north of Yorkshire. In 1830 the stagecoach was an efficient and relatively speedy way to travel; by 1850 it was effectively redundant, having been universally replaced by the railway. There was a genuine pride in this achievement. Take, for example, the opening paragraph of the section on 'Railway Stations in London' in *Bohn's Pictorial Handbook of London*:

> In the year 1830, the first railway was opened in England for steam locomotive traffic, between Liverpool and Manchester. Since that date, the progress of an invention by which time and space are nearly annihilated, has been so rapid, that at the close of the year 1850, upwards of 6,000 miles of railway were open to public use in the United Kingdom. The history of the development of this source of improved means of intercommunication has been attended with many sad episodes, and it may recall to many the recollections of bitter deceptions, and of heavy losses; but, as far as the public alone is concerned, the result of the labours of the last 20 years has been unquestionably to endow the country with one of the most powerful and efficient means of civilization.

The 'sad episodes' to which the guide refers are not railway accidents, or the injuries endured by the heroic navvies who had actually built the system, but the 'bitter deceptions' which attended railway speculation. Fortunes had been made and lost and many small investors had been ruined. This was the stuff of many Victorian novels (think for example of the arch-speculator Augustus Melmotte in Anthony Trollope's *The Way We Live Now*).

Dickens, who was not inclined to make an issue of the speculation in railway shares in his novels, was none the less a man who delighted in the benefits the railway brought. After he had made his first railway journey in 1838 he became an avid traveller. His later tours around Britain, as a celebrity public reader of his own work, would have been impossible without steam locomotives and once he had acquired Gad's Hill Place in Kent he became a regular commuter from Higham Station to London. As the wonderful essay 'A Flight' (1851) delightfully shows, he took immense pleasure in the now speedy, and to him magical, journey from London Bridge Station to a steam packet at Dover and then on to a French train to Paris. Although he seems to have been particularly prone to accidents on the line, and at one time lost part of the manuscript of *Our Mutual Friend* after a serious derailment at Staplehurst, Dickens seems to have relished both the sensation of travelling at speed and the regular rhythm of a train. In another wonderful essay, 'Railway Dreaming' (1856), he speaks of 'rattling along' in a railway carriage in a state of 'luxurious confusion': 'I take it for granted I am coming from somewhere, and going somewhere else. I seek to know no more.'

Although relatively few of Dickens's characters travel by rail (most of his Londoners seem wedded to the rhythms of a pedestrian), one novel in particular celebrates the impact of the railway on London. The London and Birmingham railway (later the London and North Western) established its London terminus at Euston Square in 1837–8. The old station, with its celebrated granite Doric 'arch' (or propylaeum), was, alas, demolished in the 1960s, but the singularly impressive cutting that brought the line southwards from Camden Town survives. It would have been hard to expunge it. It still does its job and it offers clear evidence of

'Excavations near Camden Town'. This lithograph by John Cooke Bourne (published in 1839) powerfully suggests the huge engineering works associated with the London and Birmingham Railway. This is the likely site of Dickens's Staggs's Gardens in *Dombey and Son*

what a great feat of engineering it was. Vast acres of land were acquired by the railway company, and, apart from the great cutting, the land was developed as warehouses, goods yards, engine sheds and sidings. In the process of realizing these great works, Dickens's former school, the Wellington House Academy in the Hampstead Road, lost its school room.

Dickens does not appear to mourn the loss. In *Dombey and Son* (1846–7) he instead marvels at the transformation of a great swathe of inner north-west London. Gone were physical reminders of his schooldays, gone were some pretty villas near Regent's Park and gone too were some ramshackle houses in an area that he names Staggs's Gardens:

> There was no such place as Staggs's Gardens. It had vanished from the earth. Where the old rotten summer-houses once had stood, palaces now reared their heads, and granite columns of gigantic girth opened a vista of the railway world beyond. The miserable waste ground … was swallowed up and gone; and in its frowsy stead were tiers of warehouses, crammed with rich goods and costly merchandise. The old by-streets now swarmed with passengers and vehicles of every kind; the new streets that had stopped disheartened in the mud and wagon-ruts, formed towns within themselves, originating wholesome comforts and conveniences belonging to themselves, and never tried nor thought of until they sprung into existence. Bridges that had led to nothing now led to villas, gardens, churches, healthy public walks. The carcasses of houses, beginnings of new thoroughfares, had started off upon the line at steam's own speed, and shot away into the country in a monster train …
>
> To and from the heart of this great change, all day and night, throbbing currents rushed and returned incessantly like its life's blood. Crowds of people and mountains of goods, departing and arriving scores upon scores of times in every four-and-twenty hours, produced a fermentation in the place that was always in action.

This then is a working railway station that never ceases working, and around it part of London has been utterly transformed. The

Charles Dickens Museum

Mornington Place, Hampstead Road, *c.* 1900. This shows the site of the Wellington House Academy, where Dickens went to school. The school room was lost in the late 1830s with the construction of the London and Birmingham Railway

straggling and unfinished streets and squares of the northern part of Bloomsbury now have an incentive to stretch out towards the station, while to its north new commercial and residential developments are vitally interlinked. Dickens finds a poetry in writing thus about London. This is not the ancient jumble of the City, or the fetid courtyards and alleys of Saffron Hill, or the pompous stateliness of Belgravia, but a newly regenerated London, one embracing a dynamic which is both present and future.

If Mr Podsnap had directed his hapless foreign guest to look for evidences of the 'British Constitution' in the streets around Euston Station that poor foreigner might have found himself more enlightened. Victorian London could strike visitors as stupendous as well as stupefying. For Dickens, London was a city not of stark contrasts, but of an extraordinary variety and energy. From the very beginning of his career as a writer he knew he had a distinctive vocation, and that vocation was to articulate the phenomenon that was London. Like the steam engines that he described gliding 'like tame dragons' into Euston, the metropolis that he depicted in his fiction was 'dilating with secret knowledge of great powers yet unsuspected ... and strong purposes not yet achieved'.

CHAPTER TWO

London by Foot

According to the Authorized Version of the Bible the city of Nineveh, to which the prophet Jonah was sent in order to warn of its impending destruction, was 'an exceeding great city of three days' journey'. This statement, which is possibly just a figure of speech, implies that ancient Nineveh was so sprawling a city that it took three days to walk across it. If this was indeed the case it is small wonder that Jonah proved to be such an unwilling prophet of doom. Apart from the problem of slogging his way across the city in order to find an appropriate public place from which to address its recalcitrant citizens, he would probably have found it singularly difficult to make his voice heard above the raucous buzz that still characterizes the day-to-day life of great cities.

At the end of the Book of Jonah Nineveh and its six score thousand inhabitants are spared destruction, but the account of the 'wickedness' of this ancient city very probably struck a vivid chord in the hearts of many of Dickens's scripture-minded contemporaries. By the mid-nineteenth century London had already surpassed biblical Nineveh both in extent and in population. With its unprecedented size had come unprecedented social problems which in turn had given rise to an unprecedented wickedness. Ancient Nineveh had once prospered as modern London continued to do, but by the 1840s only the shattered walls of palaces marked its abandoned site. Its ruins were explored and plundered by Dickens's friend, Sir Henry Layard. Victorian Londoners were certainly familiar enough with the results of Layard's archaeological excavations, for his spectacular finds were exhibited in the British Museum. The famous sculptures of giant human-headed bulls were for some time displayed in the museum's portico, there being insufficient room for them inside. When Layard published his economically priced *Popular Account of the Discoveries at Nineveh* in 1851 some 14,000 copies sold within weeks, many of them from railway station bookstalls.

It was not just the remains of Nineveh that haunted Victorian imaginations. Many thoughtful people firmly believed that history could, and did, repeat itself. In the first volume of his *The Stones of Venice* (also published in 1851) John Ruskin suggested that the British Empire might eventually share the destinies of Tyre and Venice and melt into maritime oblivion. Size, substance and success offered no assurances of lasting security. The fate of Nineveh, some Victorians assumed, might ultimately be shared by London.

Echoing Footsteps

The three days it may have taken to cross ancient Nineveh was probably based on the ambling pace of an Assyrian pedestrian and not on the speed of the light-weight chariots shown in the stone reliefs brought to London by Sir Henry Layard. In terms of public transport, however, not much had changed in the millennia that stretched between the fall of Nineveh and the rise of modern London in the seventeenth and eighteenth centuries. Both were, for the most part, pedestrian cities. Only the rich could afford to maintain a horse and carriage. Nevertheless, there had been hackney coaches for hire in London since the seventeenth century (and Dickens vividly described a coach stand in one of his earliest *Sketches by 'Boz'* in 1835). A three-horse public omnibus service was introduced in 1829 but only two such buses were offering a regular service between the City and Bayswater at the beginning of Queen Victoria's reign. London's first railway serving the suburbs, the London and Greenwich, only opened in December 1836.

A London omnibus, c. 1860. This comic stereo-scopic photograph suggests the logistical problems caused by the fashion for crinolines. It also offers a rare glimpse of a horse-drawn omnibus in use

The London that Dickens knew as a boy and as a young man had, therefore, only minimal public transport. Moreover, the fares charged were beyond the means of many ordinary Londoners. (In 1831 cabs charged a shilling for the first mile travelled and sixpence for every half mile thereafter; omnibuses charged sixpence for a short distance in 1837.) Most people walked to and from work. The first commuters were walkers and the distances they covered were long by modern standards. As London grew in the opening years of the nineteenth century, so the distances between home and work increased. In *A Christmas Carol* Bob Cratchit seems to think nothing of walking from Camden Town to Scrooge's counting house off Cornhill in the City; in *Great Expectations* Mr Wemmick goes on foot from Walworth through the southern suburbs of London to Little Britain; and in Dickens's

last completed novel, *Our Mutual Friend*, Reginald Wilfer regularly walks the 3 miles from his house in Holloway to Chicksey,
Veneering and Stobbles's office near Mincing Lane. Dickens's
novels are full of perambulating Londoners. None of them takes
three days to cross the city, but equally none of them can afford
either to take a cab or to amble. They all move purposefully and
with an end in sight.

None of Dickens's characters knew London as well as the
novelist himself. No one walked its high roads and its streets and
lanes as much, and as avidly, as he did. His fascination with the city,
its thoroughfares and its by-ways was established early on in his life.
London seems to have inspired him much as the poet William
Wordsworth insisted that the open fells and lakes of Westmoreland
had inspired him. Dickens's first biographer, John Forster, recalled
the novelist telling him how, as a boy, 'the cupola of St Paul's
looming through the smoke, was a treat that served him for hours
of vague reflection afterwards'. Forster goes on to describe Dickens's
delight in London's innate contrasts as he walked from suburban
Camden Town towards the city centre.

> To be taken out for a walk in the real town, especially if it were
> anywhere about Covent-garden or the Strand, perfectly
> entranced him with pleasure. But, most of all, he had a profound
> attraction of repulsion to St Giles's. If he could only induce
> whomsoever took him out to take him through Seven-dials, he
> was supremely happy.

His perambulations of London's seedier purlieus, such as the
notorious slums of St Giles's, were not always as conducive to
supreme happiness, however. As a twelve-year-old boy, unwillingly
employed pasting labels on bottles of Warren's Blacking, Dickens
had trudged daily from lodgings in Little College Street, Camden
Town, via the Hampstead Road, Tottenham Court Road and St
Martin's Lane to Warren's Warehouse at Hungerford Stairs off the
Strand. By his own account, he spent what little money he had on
stale pastries displayed on half-price trays outside confectioners'
shops or on a slice of pudding from a shop in a court behind

Hungerford Stairs, 1814. This watercolour by George Shepherd is perhaps the finest surviving visual record of the area where Dickens worked as a 'drudge' at Warren's Blacking Warehouse. It is shown at low tide. The Old Fox to the right of the picture was later taken over as Jonathan Warren's premises where the 'old grey rats' swarmed down in the cellars. The counting house, Dickens tells us, was 'on the first floor, looking over the coal barges and the river'. In *David Copperfield* the Micawber family lodge in the White Swan, 'a little, dirty, tumble-down public-house', before they set sail for Australia. This whole area was cleared in 1830 for the construction of the short-lived Hungerford Market, a building which in turn disappeared when Charing Cross Station was built in 1864

St Martin-in-the-Fields. This court was almost certainly the eccentrically named Porridge Island, demolished in 1829 to make way for improvements to St Martin's churchyard. Nevertheless, as Dickens's account of similar walks in *David Copperfield* suggests, 'the attraction of repulsion' proved to be an intensely creative process. Even in times of personal misery the close observation of London street life served to feed and nourish his fertile imagination.

According to his eldest son, the adult Dickens's walking pace was a 'regular four-miles-an-hour swing'. As he walked, his son adds, he lapsed into silence, 'the silence of engrossing thought'. Another occasional companion on such long walks, George Augustus Sala, records that Dickens was a familiar figure all over London, a man remarkable for his ubiquity.

> The omnibus conductors knew him, the street boys knew him … Elsewhere he would make his appearance in the oddest places, and in the most inclement weather: in Ratcliff Highway, on Haverstock Hill, on Camberwell Green, in Gray's Inn Road, in the Wandsworth Road, at Hammersmith Broadway, in Norton Folgate, and at Kensal New Town.

Anyone with a sense of the sprawl of modern London will recognize that Sala has selected roads at the extremes of the north, the south, the east and the west of Victorian London. Dickens got everywhere, and he got there on foot.

The Haunted City

Dickens's regular perambulations of the metropolis took place in all seasons and at all times of the day. Several of his wonderful essays, collected as *The Uncommercial Traveller* and *Reprinted Pieces*, vividly recall his restless pacing of the London streets and his acute observation of the peculiarities of the men and women he encountered. In 'City of London Churches', for example, he recounts a series of Sunday pilgrimages 'in the gentle rain or the bright sunshine' in order to explore 'that singular silence which belongs to resting-places usually astir, in scores of buildings at the heart of the world's metropolis, unknown to far greater numbers of people speaking the English tongue, than the ancient edifices of the Eternal City, or the Pyramids of Egypt'. Not all of his expeditions are as purposeful as those described in 'City of London Churches', but the London he discovers continues to enthral and inspire him. He refrains from 'sightseeing' in the conventional sense of the term. His contemporary, the French poet Charles Baudelaire, was famous as a *flâneur*, a wandering denizen of the Paris boulevards, at one with the crowds and yet detached from them. The Dickens of the essay 'Night Walks' characterizes himself as more of a tramp than a Baudelairean sophisticate. According to the essay Dickens sought to share the experiences of a singular but restless vagrant, one who is essentially urban rather than urbane. In 'Night Walks' Dickens describes a series of meandering night rambles occasioned by 'a temporary inability to sleep'. During these rambles he claims to have 'finished [his] education in a fair amateur experience of houselessness' and even adopts the temporary pseudonym 'Houselessness'. He is a shadow pursuing shadows:

> Walking the streets under the pattering rain, Houselessness would walk and walk and walk, seeing nothing but the interminable tangle of streets, save at a corner, here and there, two policemen in conversation, or the sergeant or inspector looking after his men. Now and then in the night – but rarely – Houselessness would become aware of a furtive head peering out of a doorway a few yards before him, and, coming up with the head, would find a man standing bolt upright to keep within the doorway's shadow, and evidently intent upon no particular service to society. Under a kind of fascination, and in a ghostly silence suitable to the time, Houselessness and this gentleman would eye one another from head to foot, and so, without exchange of speech, part, mutually suspicious. Drip, drip, drip, from ledge and coping, splash from pipes and water-spouts and by-and-by the houseless shadow would fall upon the stones that pave the way to Waterloo-bridge … The wild moon and clouds were as restless as an evil conscience in a tumbled bed, and the

very shadow of the immensity of London seemed to lie oppressively upon the river.

In that extraordinary last sentence we see restless 'Houselessness' identifying himself with the circumambient city. Significantly, the city's seamier side appears to express itself as a guilty oppression. Dickens's imagined London is here a kind of nightmare: a darkling city dreaming dark and fevered dreams.

Elsewhere in his work the London that Dickens imagines is rarely quite so oppressive or so benighted. Nevertheless, for many modern readers Dickens's London seems to be typified by crowds, cacophony, mischief and mayhem. It is typified as a city pervaded by poverty and a putrescent miasma. The opening paragraphs of *Bleak House*, with their emphatic repetition of the word 'fog', may alone be responsible for the generally accepted American impression that modern London is still beset by fog (though the Sherlock Holmes stories may share some of the responsibility). The impression that Dickens set his novels in a perpetual urban twilight zone was reinforced by the wonderful illustrations provided by Gustave Doré for his very Dickensian book *London: A Pilgrimage* of 1872 (its plates are frequently reproduced in studies of Victorian life). Film-makers who seek to evoke the atmosphere of Victorian London still readily resort to images of the dome of St Paul's looming above a tangle of foggy, night-shrouded alleyways. Photographs of early Victorian London do tend to confirm the fact that the city's air was polluted by coal smoke and that distances were frequently lost in a smoky haze. Meteorological evidence also confirms the frequency of atrocious autumnal and wintry pea-soupers, but to blame Dickens for resolutely establishing the notion of London's unredeemably filthy weather is to malign him. Latter-day metropolises, such as Athens and Beijing, are just as notorious for the poor quality of their air, and San Francisco and Lima are far more likely to be lost in murky sea-mists than London is (or, perhaps, ever was).

Dickens was the first great urban novelist and he remains the greatest of London novelists. With the exception of *Hard Times*, all of his novels have a London setting. London stimulated him and

'Dudley Street, Seven Dials' from *London: A Pilgrimage* by Gustave Doré (1872). This most Dickensian of studies of London was written by the novelist's younger friend Blanchard Jerrold with illustrations by the great French engraver, Doré. The artist seems to have been attracted by the gloom of London and most of his pictures give the impression that the city was perpetually twilit and shrouded in fog. This illustration shows second-hand shops in Dudley Street, known until 1845 as Monmouth Street. It had been the subject of one of Dickens's early *Sketches*. It disappeared when Shaftesbury Avenue was constructed in the 1880s

when he was cut off from its perpetual bustle he often felt lost and deracinated. John Forster records Dickens's 'craving' for London streets when he was trying to write *The Chimes* during an extended stay in Genoa in 1844. Dickens had complained to him of being 'dumbfounded' by a lack of urban vitality. 'Put me down on Waterloo-bridge at eight o'clock in the evening, with leave to roam about as long as I like, and I would come home, as you know, panting to go on. I am sadly strange as it is and can't settle.' This is far more than a statement of what is known as 'writer's block'. It is a longing, even in as busy a city as Genoa, for the familiar.

But for Dickens what was familiar about London was continually conditioned by the *unfamiliar*. London's variety, its unpredictability and its essential uncanniness seem to have echoed something deep in his own character. They also help to explain much of his creativity. Two years later, when Dickens was living in Switzerland, he again found himself confronted by a difficulty in writing, this time *Dombey and Son*. Again he wrote to Forster:

> Invention, thank God, seems the easiest thing in the world ... But the difficulty of going on at what I call a rapid pace, is prodigious; it is almost an impossibility. I suppose this is partly the effect of two years' ease, and partly of the absence of streets and numbers of figures. I can't express how much I want these. It seems as if they supplied something to my brain, which it cannot bear, when busy, to lose. For a week or a fortnight I can write prodigiously in a retired place ... and a day in London sets me up again and starts me. But the toil and labour of writing, day after day, without that magic lantern is IMMENSE!! ... My figures seem disposed to stagnate without crowds about them.

London not only 'sets him up', it somehow provides him with an imaginative projection of the kind that Dickens likens to a magic lantern. It both gives his creativity a firm footing and takes him out of himself. It both settles and unsettles. The London that Dickens missed when he was in Genoa and Switzerland was not a city clogged and befuddled by foggy darkness and mystery, it was vividly textured, multi-layered, crowded and animated.

London in Dickens's Early Fiction

PICKWICK PAPERS

By considering the very varied picture of London given in Dickens's first three novels, *Pickwick Papers* (1836–7), *Oliver Twist* (1837–9) and *Nicholas Nickleby* (1838–9) it will be possible to suggest why he found the metropolis quite so creatively stimulating. It may also help readers to understand how vital Dickens's role was in transforming the relatively new and troubling phenomenon of a world city into the substance of art. Although all three early novels contain important sections set outside the capital, and each also describes a journey, or journeys, to and from London, in their very different ways all three vividly represent the expanding, hard-nosed, frenetic and dingy London of the late 1820s and 1830s. This was the London which seems to have enthralled and appalled visitors in equal measure. As we have seen in the first chapter, it was a metropolis that was both physically reconstructing itself and, to a large degree, redefining itself. Dickens's fiction was integrally bound up with this process of redefinition.

Despite the fact that a good deal of *Pickwick Papers* is taken up with the stage-coach expeditions of the Pickwick Club through the southern, western and midland counties of England, the club and its chairman are based in London. Samuel Pickwick is an out-and-out Cockney, a Londoner to his finger-tips. Indeed, one of the first things that readers learn about him is that he is resident in Goswell Street and that when he looked out of his bedroom window 'Goswell-street was at his feet, Goswell-street was on the right hand – as far as the eye could reach, Goswell-street extended on his left, and the opposite side of Goswell-street was over the way'. Goswell Street (now Goswell Road) leads northwards from the City of London to the once suburban purlieus of Islington. It was a long, undistinguished residential street lined with solid three-storey late Georgian terraced houses and it seemed to provide Mr Pickwick with a serene frame of mind and an assured Cockney sense of self-containment. 'As well might I be content to gaze on Goswell-street for ever,' Pickwick asserts, 'without one effort to penetrate to the hidden counties which on every side surround it.' The weather on the sunlit May morning in 1827 when the novel opens is evidently fine enough for him not only to see across the street, but up and down it as well. Here at least there is no sign of fog.

In Chapter 12 we learn far more about his accommodation:

Mr Pickwick's apartments in Goswell-street, although on a limited scale, were not only of a very neat and comfortable description, but peculiarly adapted for the residence of a man of his genius and observation. His sitting-room was the first floor front, his bedroom the second floor front; and thus, whether he were sitting at his desk in the parlour, or standing before the dressing-glass in his dormitory, he had an equal opportunity of contemplating human nature in all the phases it exhibits, in that popular thoroughfare.

Charles Dickens Museum

Windsor Terrace, City Road, c. 1920. The residence of Mr Micawber in *David Copperfield*. Here David has a room 'at the top of the house, at the back ... very scantily furnished'. Here too Mrs Micawber endeavours to establish her Boarding Academy for Young Ladies. This photograph shows us a typical aspect of the Islington that Dickens knew well. Mr Pickwick would have lived in a very similar house in Goswell Street

Pickwick has selected what was known as a 'front pair' of rooms in the house tenanted by his landlady, the widowed Mrs Bardell. It is she who provides most of the domestic necessities for her two lodgers (the other lodger is 'a large man' who is evidently content with the 'back pair' of rooms; Mrs Bardell and her young son must have confined themselves to the basement and ground floor rooms). Despite the fact that we are told that 'cleanliness and quiet reigned throughout the house', Pickwick seems to prefer the street because, despite the dust of a busy thoroughfare and the rattle of horse-drawn traffic on the road below him, he can observe urban humanity as it passes by. Dickens has therefore introduced his central character as a single gentleman of modest means, who in his retirement from business is content with rented lodgings in a respectable but far from fashionable area of London. The Pickwick of the early numbers of the novel is an observer of modern mankind and a would-be antiquarian, an early nineteenth-century *homme moyen sensuel* who is confident enough of the values of present-day urban civilization to indulge in a study of the quaintnesses of the past.

Much of the social vision of *Pickwick Papers* is conditioned by Mr Pickwick's lower middle-class bachelor perspectives on the present as much as on the past. As Dickens gradually develops his character and his milieu, Pickwick acquires a certain degree of wisdom without ever completely losing his innocence. Crucially, from Chapter 10 onwards, the novelist gives him the counterpoise offered by the practical working-class wisdom of Sam Weller, but he, like Sam, remains a quintessential modern Londoner. To an important degree, Mr Pickwick looks at provincial England as he looks at populous Goswell Street. But Pickwick's London is neither uniformly sunlit nor secure. Towards the middle of the narrative the novel takes on a new darkness. This is particularly evident in the sections concerned with Pickwick's confinement in the Fleet Prison and in the gloomy story of the 'tall, gaunt, cadaverous' Chancery prisoner. Nevertheless, in the final chapters readers are again ushered into the sunlight, into bourgeois security and into a sense of happy resolution. The Pickwick Club is dissolved, its provincial journeyings are discontinued, and Mr Pickwick retires to Dulwich, then a suburban village especially distinguished by its new art gallery (London's first public display of Old Masters, and a place in which Pickwick is 'frequently' seen contemplating the pictures). At Dulwich 'all the light clouds of the more solemn part of the proceedings' pass away and 'every face shone forth joyously'. The faces shine here as Mr Snodgrass marries in Dulwich Church and Mr Pickwick entertains the wedding guests on his lawn. Sunshine seems to have been very much in Dickens's mind. However darkly the Fleet Prison loomed earlier in the narrative, now there is 'unmixed happiness' of the kind which cheers 'our transitory existence here'.

> There are dark shadows on the earth, but its lights are stronger in the contrast. Some men, like bats, have better eyes for the darkness than for the light; we, who have no such optical powers, are better pleased to take our last parting look at the visionary companions of many solitary hours, when the brief sunshine of the world is blazing full upon them.

The 'we' here is both an authorial 'royal we' and the broad community of readers established by that author. We, like Pickwick's companions, are caught up in the benevolence that has characterized the novel's hero. It is a benevolence which has also properly been described as Dickensian.

OLIVER TWIST

Dickens began to serialize *Oliver Twist* in February 1837, when he was still in the middle of the composition of *Pickwick Papers*. The fact that he could cope with such facility with two radically different stories is testimony to his extraordinary creative energy. It is also remarkable that his two central characters should be so different, not only from one another, but also from Dickens's own immediate experience. Samuel Pickwick is a plump and ageing middle-class bachelor; Oliver Twist is an extraordinarily different creation: an orphaned boy condemned to the workhouse, then to drudgery in a provincial undertaker's shop, then to criminality. The two novels do have London in common, however. They are also thematically united by the fact that they move from darkness to light, and from the dreamlike to the nightmarish, and they end in the serenity of bourgeois London of the 1830s. In Chapter 17 of *Oliver Twist* Dickens famously compares his alternation of comic and tragic scenes to 'the layers of red and white in a side of streaky, well-cured bacon'. This 'streaky bacon' structure can in many ways be related to the very nature of contemporary London. Urban life lacked stability. Just as Mr Pickwick moves from financial security to a debtors' prison, so, even more starkly, Oliver Twist falls into association with Fagin and is rescued by Mr Brownlow, only to be dragged down again by Nancy and Sikes.

In Oliver's case it is significant that Fagin's den in Saffron Hill is less than a mile away from Mr Brownlow's pleasant house in

Charles Dickens Museum

Little Saffron Hill, *c.* 1896. An evocative view of commercial properties which would have been familiar to Dickens. The worst of the slum property had been demolished before this photograph was taken

Pentonville. As Victorian Londoners were well aware it was easy enough to wander out of areas of middle-class respectability and into some of the worst slums in Europe. The notorious St Giles's Rookery and the adjacent Seven Dials were, for example, only a short walk south of thoroughly upper-middle-class Bloomsbury (though the latter was in the nineteenth century cordoned off by gates manned by uniformed officers employed by the Duke of Bedford's estate). No such gates seemed to divide the houses around Lincoln's Inn Fields, described in *Bleak House*, from the fictional, but no less atrocious, slum of Tom-all-Alone's and there were no physical barriers between the Pentonville of *Oliver Twist* and Saffron Hill, where Dickens places Fagin's den. When the singularly naive Oliver is 'discovered' by the Artful Dodger (John Dawkins) and introduced to Fagin and his gang in Chapter 8, Dickens carefully describes the route into London taken by the two boys. It is like a spider's web:

> As John Dawkins objected to their entering London before nightfall, it was nearly eleven o'clock when they reached the turnpike at Islington. They crossed from the Angel into St John's-road; struck down the small street which terminates at Sadler's Wells Theatre; through Exmouth-street and Coppice-row; down the little court by the side of the workhouse; across the classic ground which once bore the name of Hockley-in-the-Hole; thence into Little Saffron-hill; and so into Saffron-hill the Great; along which the Dodger scudded at a rapid pace: directing Oliver to follow close at his heels … A dirtier or more wretched place he had never seen. The street was very narrow and muddy; and the air was impregnated with filthy odours … Covered ways and yards, which here and there diverged from the main street, disclosed little knots of houses, where drunken men and women were positively wallowing in the filth; and from several of the doorways, great ill-looking fellows were cautiously emerging: bound, to all appearance, on no very well-disposed or harmless errands.

This sounds very like the kind of twilit slum that Dickens would later describe in 'Night Walks'. But in *Oliver Twist* the spider at the centre of this particular web is, of course, Fagin, and one of the 'great ill-looking fellows' who lurk in doorways is probably Bill Sikes. Dickens is very precise as to how Oliver finds himself drawn into the web. What we should note, however, is not just how dreadful Saffron Hill appears to Oliver but also how in arriving there he has passed through perfectly respectable, if scarcely fashionable, areas of Islington. He has skirted close by Mr Pickwick's Goswell Street and within ½ mile of the 'neat house, in a quiet shady street near Pentonville' to which the benevolent Mr Brownlow takes him in Chapter 12. At Clerkenwell Green, roughly halfway between Pentonville and Saffron Hill, Oliver is recaptured by Sikes and dragged back 'into a labyrinth of dark narrow courts'. In *Oliver Twist*, as elsewhere in Dickens's novels, the courts and lanes of slumland stand virtually cheek by jowl with the more orderly streets and squares of middle-class inner suburbia.

Some of the stark juxtapositions of London slum and London suburb, chaos and order, darkness and light, which characterize *Oliver Twist* have been vividly reimpressed on the public imagination by

Hockley-in-the-Hole, Clerkenwell, *c.* 1900. Dickens's untidy slumland caught shortly before it disappeared in clearance schemes

David Lean's wonderful film version of the novel produced in 1948 and by the many revivals of Lionel Bart's sentimental musical *Oliver!* (which was in turn filmed in 1968 by Carol Reed).

One further *locus* must also be mentioned, and that is Newgate Prison, which figures so prominently in both the real and the imagined histories of London and Londoners. It once stood on the site of the present Central Criminal Court in Old Bailey in the City of London. Before he wrote *Oliver Twist* Dickens had already described this 'gloomy depository of the guilt and misery of London' in his 'A Visit to Newgate' in *Sketches by 'Boz'*. He memorably depicted the burning of the prison during the Gordon Riots of 1780 in his historical novel, *Barnaby Rudge* (1841), and he used the prison and its neighbouring law court again in *A Tale of Two Cities* (1859). But it is its appearance in the closing chapters of *Oliver Twist* that is the most striking and the most haunting. It is here, behind 'the dreadful walls of Newgate', that the condemned Fagin is brought, and here that the terrified prisoner awaits death by public hanging on a gallows erected in the street in front of the prison. The night before Fagin is to die Oliver and Mr Brownlow pass 'through several strong gates' and find him 'rocking from side to side, with a countenance more like that of a snared beast than the face of a man'. The oppressive gloom of the cell and Fagin's tormented face were the subject of perhaps the darkest and most disturbing of all of George Cruikshank's illustrations to the first edition of the novel. It is small wonder, therefore, that readers greet the novel's final move from darkness to light with a sense of pure relief. Day dawns as Oliver and his guardian leave the prison and everything in the outside world speaks of 'life and animation'. Even in the public street, however, the waiting gallows and the 'hideous apparatus of death' bring home both to Dickens's characters and to his readers the essential ambiguity of a London where human destinies, like human endings, can be as sticky as they can be blessed.

NICHOLAS NICKLEBY

The world of *Nicholas Nickleby* is just as confused and confusing as that of *Oliver Twist*, but the contrasts seem less stark. For the first time in his career Dickens offers his readers a young, virtuous and ambitious male hero, and he also offers a greater range of characters drawn from all sections of society. Yet again, in the chapters set in London, he explores the potential of this social range by re-exploring London character-types established by his literary forebears. His aristocrats (Sir Mulberry Hawk and Lord Frederick Verisopht) are men-about-town who ultimately derive their debauchery and their comic exaggeration from Shakespeare and from the rakish comedies written in the Restoration period. Dickens's middle-class businessmen (both the unscrupulous Ralph Nickleby and the benevolent Cheeryble brothers) could equally appear in a play by Ben Jonson, a novel by Henry Fielding or an engraving by William Hogarth. Nevertheless, there is something both distinctively Dickensian and authentically London-like in the characters drawn from less privileged social circles. The shabby gentility of Newman Noggs, for example, or the social pretensions of the Kenwigs family (despite being married to an ivory turner, Susan Kenwigs insists that she stems from a 'very genteel family') are suggestive of an acute observation of contemporary London life.

The London of *Nicholas Nickleby* is shown in a very varied light. There is a good deal of darkness, of course, as there is in *Oliver Twist*, but Dickens is less concerned to expose slumland to public view and more determined to show us work places, commercial activity and an often disconcerting animation. One of the gloomiest sites in the novel, the house selected by Ralph Nickleby as the residence of his sister-in-law and niece, is scarcely a desirable place to live but it is also decidedly not situated in a notorious slum. Spigwiffin's Wharf is Dickens's invention, and he sites it off the busy Lower Thames Street, between London Bridge and the Custom House:

> They went into the City, turning down by the river side; and after a long and very slow drive, the streets being crowded at that house with vehicles of every kind, stopped in front of a large old dingy house in Thames Street, the door and windows of which were so bespattered with mud, that it would have appeared to be uninhabited for years ...

Old and gloomy and black in truth it was, and sullen and dark were the rooms once so bustling with life and enterprise. There was a wharf behind, opening on the Thames. An empty dog-kennel, some bones of animals, fragments of iron hoops and staves of old casks, lay strewn about but no life was stirring there. It was a picture of cold, silent decay.

Naturally enough, Kate Nickleby finds it depressing and chilling, and fears that it might be haunted by the unhappy memories of 'some dreadful crime'. Thames Street must represent a real enough contrast to the cottage in rural Devon in which she had grown up. What Dickens is suggesting about the house, however, is not that it is cursed by unpleasant memories but that it has lost its commercial purpose. Thames Street is busy enough, we assume (hence the mud bespattered windows), but the economic enterprise for which the house was built has vanished. At the time of the novel's composition the wharves in the old Pool of London were losing their commercial significance as trade moved down river to the

Upper Thames Street, c. 1890. Although there has been much mid-nineteenth-century reconstruction in this photograph, Dickens would have readily recognized the street. All the buildings shown here have now been obliterated

Dove Court, c. 1900. A typical enough City backwater of the type that now so rarely survives. This is Scrooge's London, sequestered, private, decaying and now irretrievably lost

Charles Dickens Museum

expanding docks in the East End. Equally, better-off merchants and tradesmen were beginning to move their families out to the suburbs while retaining premises in the City given over exclusively to business. When in *Little Dorrit* Dickens again describes a house in this area, Mrs Clennam's 'old brick house, so dingy as to be all but black', readers are led to understand that these once grand seventeenth-century merchants' houses now represent ways of life and living that are increasingly defunct. Indeed, Mrs Clennam's house is slowly, and symbolically, collapsing, having been vainly propped up with 'half a dozen gigantic crutches'. Ralph Nickleby has evidently acquired his empty Thames-side house as an adjunct to his business empire. Though unserviceable for commerce it proves to be a convenient enough dumping ground for his unwanted relatives.

If the Thames-side area of the City was in decline, other parts of the Square Mile, as we glimpse them in *Nicholas Nickleby*, still retained some signs of real commercial energy. The Cheerybles' offices and warehouse were situated in City Square, another product of Dickens's imagination. When Nicholas Nickleby first sees it in Chapter 37, the square is described as 'a quiet, shady little square' lying somewhere between Threadneedle Street and Bishopsgate:

> The City Square has no inclosure, save the lamp-post in the middle, and no grass but the weeds which spring up round its base. It is a quiet, little-frequented, retired spot favourable to melancholy and contemplation, and appointments of long-waiting ... It is so quiet that you can almost hear the ticking of your own watch when you stop to cool in its refreshing atmosphere. There is a distant hum – of coaches, not of insects – but no other sound disturbs the stillness of the square.

Dickens seems to insist on the still coolness of City Square in order to distinguish the honest commercial enterprise of the Cheerybles from that of a businessman like Ralph Nickleby, whose premises are in the West End. Nevertheless, some early Victorian readers might have found the situation of the Cheerybles' offices almost as extraordinary as the virtue and the commercial astuteness of the brothers themselves. It is far harder for modern readers to judge, for the City was to change so radically in Dickens's lifetime and it has continued to change, with a headlong rapidity, in the century and a half since his death. As old businesses and old business methods declined, and as the surviving population of the City deserted it for the suburbs, they were replaced by larger and larger purpose-built offices. Once in a while visitors in search of relics of Dickens's London may come across surviving oases of quiet amid the gherkins and the towers of the modern City but they are rare, and precious few now survive in the region of Threadneedle Street.

In introducing City Square to readers of *Nicholas Nickleby* Dickens was equally determined to distinguish it from the kind of West End residential square with which they might have been more familiar. He specifically mentions 'the aristocratic gravity' of Grosvenor and Hanover Squares, the 'dowager barrenness and

The City of London from the Monument, c. 1857. The cramped, largely seven-teenth- and eighteenth-century townscape was still dominated by its church spires. The buildings in the foreground are, however, part of new constructions lining the approach to London Bridge. This is the City, with St Paul's receding into the fog, with which Dickens was familiar

frigidity' of Fitzroy Square and the 'gravel walks and garden seats' of Russell and Euston Squares. These references are significant for they serve to remind us that the focus has shifted westward from the north/south axis of Islington and the Borough which we met with in *Pickwick* and *Oliver Twist*. The fashionable dressmaking estab-lishment run by Madame Mantalini is, for example, housed in premises in Cavendish Square. The showroom in the saloon on the first floor is approached through a 'handsome hall, and up a spacious staircase'. Madame Mantalini's pretentious mansion is not, however, representative of the West End as we experience it in the novel. Far more typical is Ralph Nickleby's spacious house in the no longer fashionable Golden Square, immediately to the east of the relatively newly laid-out Regent Street:

> Although few members of the graver professions live about Golden Square, it is not exactly in anybody's way to or from anywhere. It is one of the squares that have been; a quarter of the town that has gone down in the world and taken to letting lodgings ... Its boarding houses are musical, and the notes of pianos and harps float in the evening time round the head of the mournful statue, the guardian genius of the little wilderness of shrubs, in the centre of the square.

A few Georgian houses survive in Golden Square, but the house believed to be the one that Dickens thought of as a proper residence for Ralph Nickleby was demolished in the early 1920s. Elsewhere in his work the streets around the square are memorable for the seedy and run-down house, let out to multiple poor tenants, in which

Golden Square, Soho, c. 1900. The square was in Dickens's time a part of London that had 'gone down in the world, and taken to letting lodgings'. In *David Copperfield* one of these tenements provides a refuge for Martha and Em'ly. Most of the old houses disappeared in the course of the twentieth century

13 Golden Square, Soho, c. 1900. This fine early eighteenth-century house was often assumed to be the house that Dickens allots to Ralph Nickleby in *Nicholas Nickleby*. It was demolished in the 1920s

Martha and Em'ly find refuge in *David Copperfield*. This whole area of western Soho is delineated from far grander Mayfair by the steady northward march of Regent Street and it has managed to retain much of its slightly seedy character. Certainly, if we look up above the façades of boutiques, shops, warehouses and cafés in Broad Street, Lexington Street or Carnaby Street it is just possible to identify the kind of house in which Newman Noggs, the Kenwigs and later Nicholas himself lodged:

> In that quarter of London in which Golden Square is situated there is a bygone, faded, tumble-down street, with two irregular rows of tall meagre houses, which seem to have stared each other out of countenance years ago. The very chimneys appear to have grown dismal and melancholy from having had nothing better to look at than the chimneys over the way. Their tops are battered, and broken, and blackened with smoke; and, here and there, some taller stack than the rest, inclining heavily to one

side and toppling over the roof, seems to meditate taking revenge for half a century's neglect by crushing the inhabitants of the garrets beneath.

This then is a part of London in which respectability just about survives amid the architectural evidence of better days and a better class of person. Here the prosperous, the aspirant and the poor live jumbled together in a tangle of streets which never seem to quite connect with one another and which often peter out into alleys and courtyards. Just as much as the City, or the Inns of Court, or Saffron Hill or Seven Dials, this is quintessentially Dickens's London.

In many significant ways the physical fabric of Dickens's London is lost to us. The lines of streets, major monuments and certain historically charged enclaves, such as the Temple or Lincoln's Inn, survive largely intact and would be readily recognized by a time-travelling original reader of Dickens's novels. Otherwise redevelopment, demolition, air raids and 'urban renewal' have taken their dire toll. London is not necessarily more interesting or more elegant because of the changes but it is certainly cleaner, healthier, better lit and tidier. Its citizens are better housed and it can generally be proud of the development of its public transport. Londoners, and visitors to London, still determinedly walk its streets, but they do so less assiduously than their Victorian predecessors and they certainly miss many of the details of London history that manage to survive. Prophets of doom still wander through the metropolis, much as Jonah did as he crossed the sprawling city of Nineveh. But, unlike Nineveh, the modern Babylon continues to flourish.

The London that readers of Dickens encounter in his fiction is both real and unreal, both factual and imagined. Some of his admirers feel that they know his London without even visiting it. Others feel a familiar glow when they first encounter surviving aspects of it, and yet others seek its fogs, its demolished prisons and its night-shrouded slum alleys in vain. A later novel than the ones we have been concentrating on in this section, *Bleak House* (1852–3), can be said to exemplify the complex admixture of fact and fiction, the observed and the imagined, that characterizes

Dean Street, Soho, c. 1900. A classic Soho street full of 'irregular rows of tall meagre houses'. This is the world of Newman Noggs and the Kenwigs in *Nicholas Nickleby*

Dickens's best work. Those topographical explorers who choose to look can still find virtually intact many of the sites around Lincoln's Inn Fields, Chancery Lane, Soho Square and Fitzrovia described in the novel, and they can move around them much as his characters did, but no one has ever found or will ever find the 'neighbouring' Tom-all-Alone's. Dickens's festering slum never existed anywhere except in his imagination and even its name is pure invention. Dickens stretches and exaggerates truth and, throughout his work, he consistently transforms the evidence of nineteenth-century London. That was what his peculiar genius equipped him to do. Dickens's London is best encountered in his fiction, but aspects of his London can still also be thrillingly, and sometimes unexpectedly, discovered in its modern streets.

CHAPTER THREE

Dickens in Legal Land: Inns and Prisons

ICKENS GENERALLY HAD no love for lawyers. There were exceptions in his private life, but his novels consistently reveal a collection of conniving, hypocritical, pompous, secretive, manipulative, self-seeking, fuddy-duddy and even dishonest men of the law. His prejudices against the profession probably began when, soon after leaving school, the fifteen-year-old Dickens began work as a junior clerk in the offices of Ellis and Blackmore. These offices were then in 'a poor old set of chambers of three rooms' in Holborn Court, which now forms part of South Square, in Gray's Inn. Some sixth months after he began work the offices moved to the second floor of the newly built Raymond Buildings. It was, however, at 2 Holborn Court that Dickens would later locate Tommy Traddles's chambers in *David Copperfield*. The generous-minded Traddles is, we should remember, that real rarity among Dickens's characters, a barrister 'with a rising reputation among the lawyers'. Nevertheless, when David mounts the rickety staircase to visit him in Chapter 59 he puts his foot in a hole 'where the Honorable Society of Gray's Inn had left a plank deficient' and falls head over heels.

David's accident may suggest to us that Gray's Inn was determined to assert its dilapidated, inconvenient and inhospitable nature. Certainly Dickens elsewhere expresses little appreciation of its architecture, of its then current decay or of what he saw as its

Charles Dickens Museum

Gray's Inn Hall, c. 1900. All of these buildings disappeared during the Second World War

equally seedy inhabitants. This is how he describes it in the *Uncommercial Traveller* essay 'Chambers' (1860):

I look upon Gray's Inn generally as one of the most depressing institutions in brick and mortar, known to the children of men. Can anything be more dreary than its arid Square, Sahara Desert of the law, with the ugly old tiled-topped tenements, the dirty windows, the bills To Let, To Let, the door-posts inscribed like gravestones, the crazy gateway giving upon the filthy Lane, the scowling iron-barred prison-like passage into Verulam-buildings, the mouldy red-nosed ticket-porters with little coffin plates, and why with aprons, the dry hard atomy-like appearance of the whole dust-heap? When my uncommercial travels tend to this dismal spot, my comfort is its rickety state. Imagination gloats over the fulness of time, when the staircases shall have quite tumbled down – they are daily wearing into an ill-savoured powder, but have not quite tumbled down yet – when the last prolix old bencher all of the olden time, shall have been got out of an upper window by means of a Fire-Ladder, and carried off to the Holborn Union … Then shall a squalid little trench, with rank grass and a pump in it, lying between the coffee-house and South-square, be wholly given up to cats and rats, and not, as now, have its empire divided between those animals and a few briefless bipeds – surely called to the Bar by voices of deceiving spirits, seeing that they are wanted there by no mortal – who glance down, with eyes better glazed than their casements, from their dreary and lacklustre rooms.

Despite Traddles's singularly jolly tenancy of his cramped chambers in Holborn Court, Dickens clearly had no affection either for what Gray's Inn looked like or for what it stood for. Indeed, such was his antipathy that he repeats phrases from the essay in the diatribe against the neighbouring and equally 'dismal' Barnard's Inn which he gives to Pip in Chapter 2 of the second book of *Great Expectations*. If anything, Gray's Inn in the 1820s resembled a particularly decrepit and undistinguished Cambridge college where superannuated bachelor dons clung on to their fellowships until death released them into a different state of dust. Dickens knew little about contemporary, unreformed Cambridge, but he certainly knew the backwaters of the English legal establishment and he was decidedly unsympathetic to it. He would probably not have mourned the fact that so much of the historic core of Gray's Inn was destroyed by bombing in the Second World War. The plain brick range of Raymond Buildings of 1825, however, survives intact, as do the fine gardens behind. In *Little Dorrit* the gushing Flora Finching reminds Arthur Clennam that he had once walked out with her on the north-west side of these gardens 'at exactly four o'clock in the afternoon'. The remembrance doesn't appear to cheer the melancholy Arthur.

In Chancery

Despite the fact that so many of his bachelor and newly married characters happily rent convenient and economical chambers in the various Inns of Court, Dickens generally seems to associate the inns themselves with decay, delay, inefficacy and unfruitfulness. These are problems he also readily associates with the English legal system of his time. The four surviving great inns, Gray's, Lincoln's, and the Middle and Inner Temple, were supplemented in Dickens's day by minor institutions, the Inns of Chancery, which had historically been either related or attached to the greater ones. These secondary institutions had very commonly lost their legal identity in Dickens's time and been taken over as residences by private and professional families. Some of their buildings, such as Staple Inn and Barnard's Inn in Holborn, still exist, albeit in truncated form. Others, such as Clement's Inn in the Strand, or Furnival's and Thavies Inns in Holborn or Serjeants' and Symond's Inns, both once in Chancery Lane, survive only as names. Nearly all appear in Dickens's novels, often in a memorably melancholy manner.

Clifford's Inn, c. 1900. The Inn had been rebuilt in 1767–8. It was sold in 1903 and in 1911 it was acquired by the Society of Knights Bachelor. It was demolished in 1934 and replaced by offices

Charles Dickens Museum

Clifford's Inn, *c.* 1900. The Inn before it was demolished in 1934. Its garden just about survives nowadays; otherwise the name of the Inn is its only real memorial

These generally undistinguished architectural expressions of the legal establishment occupied a great swathe of land to the west of the City of London that stretched from the River Thames in the south to the north side of Holborn. Any glance at a map of London in Dickens's time will suggest the extent to which they dominated the life of the very centre of the metropolis, but they dominated it modestly and undemonstratively, screened from public scrutiny behind closed gates. The fact that each of the inns was independent and that each held the freehold on its properties has meant that, despite extensive bomb-damage in the 1940s, a great number of historic structures, and equally historic open spaces, have survived into the twenty-first century. Only the monumental Gothic-revival Royal Courts of Justice in the Strand, designed on a 7-acre site by G. E. Street in 1871–2, now intrude into areas which would be readily familiar to Dickens. The Law Courts have, since they moved here in the years following Dickens's death from buildings adjacent to Westminster Hall, reinforced the idea that this central area is emphatically 'legal London'.

For Dickens, 'legal London' was an anomalous encumbrance rather than an enhancement of the well-being of the capital. Readers of *Bleak House*, much of the action of which is set in the area, are likely to be well aware of Dickens's prejudices. The first monthly part, published in March 1852, opened with a famously gloomy evocation of the great city at its autumnal dreariest:

> London. Michaelmas term lately over and the Lord Chancellor sitting in Lincoln's Inn Hall. Implacable November weather. As much mud in the streets, as if the waters were but newly retired form the face of the earth, and it would not be wonderful to meet a Megalosaurus, forty feet long or so, waddling like an elephan- tine lizard up Holborn Hill.

London is bogged down in fog and mud. The mud is so pervasive that at a once notoriously inconvenient section of Holborn, just

Lincoln's Inn Hall and Chapel, 1830. This engraving by Thomas H. Shepherd shows Old Square and the medieval Hall in which the Court of Chancery is sitting at the opening of *Bleak House*. Kenge and Carboy have their offices in Old Square

beyond Furnival's Inn, it would not be surprising to encounter one of the beasts from the primeval morass, a megalosaurus, a 'great lizard', which had been so named some twenty-five years earlier by the naturalist, William Buckland. Dickens's images are of Noah's flood, newly retreated, and of an antediluvian monster. The first image might imply hope and a new beginning, but the megalosaurus seems to threaten a return to an earlier phase of creation. What Dickens seems to be suggesting is that all of human civilization is threatened with regression. Modern London is clogged with mud underfoot while its air is polluted with fog, smoke and a disease-bearing miasma. Without change and reform, the city's future seems bleak indeed.

Holborn Hill was a hill because it formed the west bank of the now lost River Fleet. A key traffic artery was thus forced to descend down a slope into the valley of the Fleet and then climb up again as it approached the City. The traffic problems were only alleviated in 1869 with the construction of Holborn Viaduct, London's first, and certainly most grandiose, 'flyover'. The extensive building works associated with Holborn Viaduct not only removed the inconveniences described by Dickens, they also finally drove underground the dirty ditch which was still designated the 'River' Fleet, and they destroyed many of the ramshackle houses in the Saffron Hill area which sprawled on its western banks.

As both *Oliver Twist* and *Bleak House* suggest to us, the 'legal London' of magistrates' courts and inns of court stood cheek by jowl with pockets of urban poverty and the notorious haunts of criminals. Respectability and the law were only a matter of streets away from dereliction and delinquency. Moreover, in *Bleak House*, the fog that pollutes the air and the mud underfoot are integrally linked to the chaos inspired by a complex, befuddled and befuddling legal system, one exemplified in the novel by the painfully slow workings of the Court of Chancery ('at the very heart of the fog, sits the Lord High Chancellor in his High Court of Chancery'). At the beginning of the novel, the Court of Chancery is sitting in the old hall of Lincoln's Inn. It sat there out of session rather than in Westminster Hall. Dickens therefore places the 'legal London' that stretches from the Temple in the south to Holborn in the north at the topographical

Fleet Street in the early 1860s. We are looking towards St Martin's, Ludgate, with St Paul's looming through the haze beyond it. This photograph was taken before the London, Chatham and Dover Railway built its (now vanished) viaduct over the bottom of Ludgate Hill in 1865

Charles Dickens Museum

heart of his story. Through this territory run central London's two great west-east arteries: Holborn and, south of it, the Strand and Fleet Street. In Dickens's time these two great streets were regularly blocked by traffic. Progress along Holborn was, as we have seen, impeded by the problems of Holborn Hill, while between the Strand and Fleet Street stood Temple Bar, the ceremonial gate to the City of London, and a notorious bottleneck for wheeled vehicles. For Dickens the sclerosis inherent in the blockages of two great London thoroughfares represents the way in which the unreformed law impedes the progress of the nation.

Despite the dignity accorded to Temple Bar by the City of London, the arch was neither particularly admired nor especially honoured by early Victorian Londoners. One guidebook of the 1850s noted that it was 'far from possessing anything remarkable or even graceful'. Most people seem to have thought of it as an incumbrance. On the raw afternoon when *Bleak House* begins we are told that 'the dense fog is densest, and the muddy streets are muddiest, near the leaden-headed old obstruction: Temple Bar', while at the opening of Book Two of A Tale of Two Cities readers are reminded that the nearby Tellson's Bank always has its windows 'under a shower-bath of mud from Fleet-street'. Temple Bar, which casts its 'heavy' shadow over the bank's premises, was, Dickens insists, still gorily decorated with the rotten heads of Jacobites condemned after the 1745 rebellion (A Tale of Two Cities is set in the 1780s). The heads were long gone by the time Dickens wrote the novel, but Temple Bar itself survived until it was taken down in 1878 in order to facilitate the construction of the new Royal Courts of Justice. Having been removed and rebuilt as a hefty garden ornament on a Hertfordshire estate it finally returned to London in the opening years of the twenty-first century. No attempt was made to put it back on its original site (London's traffic had got too used to its not being in the Strand). It was reconstructed on land to the north of St Paul's, where it looks elegant enough, if incongruously deracinated.

Stagnation v Circulation

With the Strand literally 'barred' and Holborn bemired in mud it cannot surprise readers of Bleak House that the London of the novel was coming to a standstill and that the wider world beyond was having to endure the consequences. The fog, the mud, the inadequacies of the administration and, above all, the law's delays, were strangling the capital. The disinclination to change anything is evident in London's mid-Victorian street plan. Contemporary maps of the growing metropolis reveal quite how important Holborn and the Strand/Fleet Street were as the major links between the residential and administrative West End and the commercial and industrial areas of the City and Docklands. The River Thames was still in active use, but, as London had expanded northwards and westwards, the tidal river was not always the most efficient and reliable of thoroughfares. In the 1810s John Nash had brought about radical changes in the planning of the residential and commercial West End but next to nothing had been done to relieve the congestion east of Charing Cross. Nash had redeveloped Crown land, but elsewhere in London the problem lay in the hands of a multitude of private landowners and self-satisfied institutions. Thanks to the nature of national government and the virtual absence of efficient local administration, nineteenth-century London lacked the kind of imperial planning *diktats* that changed the face of Paris, rendered Berlin a good place to march through and kept St Petersburg elegant and disciplined. In the names of liberty and representative government England had indifference and vested interest.

As we have seen 'legal London' effectively blocked any further opening up of central London. Blackfriars Bridge had opened in 1769 and, to the west of it, Waterloo Bridge in 1817, but between them no bridge could cross the Thames because the rambling courts and ranges of the Temple occupied much of the north bank. Even

Lincoln's Inn Gateway, Chancery Lane, *c.* 1890. The gateway was reconstructed in 1966–9

the superb span of the old Waterloo Bridge led to a virtual dead-end in Dickens's day. A traveller from south London crossing the bridge would turn into Wellington Street (where he passed the offices of Dickens's journal *All the Year Round*), but once Wellington Street had merged with Bow Street it stopped its northward progress at Long Acre. East of Lincoln's Inn, the narrow and inconvenient Chancery Lane would scarcely have struck any Londoner as an inviting or felicitous alternative route. For historical rather than geographical reasons, therefore, this important part of central London simply had no major north/south arteries.

At the very heart of knotted, congested Dickensian London stood Lincoln's Inn and its adjacent fields. It was small wonder that Dickens set so much of the action of *Bleak House* here. Even today, if we were to draw a Union Jack on a map of modern London, Lincoln's Inn Fields would lie at the core. This area, an axis and a mid-point between the City and Westminster, is a largely unacknowledged and unconsidered core. London had to wait until the very end of the nineteenth century before a solution was found. This entailed the wholesale demolition of scores of seventeenth- and eighteenth-century properties in the area around Wych Street and the bottom of Drury Lane. These prop-erties were reconstructed in the heavy Edwardian Baroque style when the arc of the Aldwych came into being and when a great new thoroughfare, Kingsway, pushed its way northwards between Covent Garden and Lincoln's Inn Fields. Though long planned, work only began on this grandiose scheme in 1900 and despite the fact that many of the new buildings were unfinished, Kingsway was opened in 1905 by King Edward VII (in whose honour the new street was named). The old houses in Wych Street and Drury Lane were not much mourned in the 1890s, though a group of far-sighted antiquarians did record the streets just before they vanished. Led by the photographer Henry Dixon of the Society for Photographing Relics of Old London, a series of memorable and beautiful photographic plates was produced. They form the finest record we have of a unique and irreplaceable part of London.

Tom-all-Alone's and Wych Street

The demolition of the old wooden houses in Wych Street deprived latter-day readers of Dickens of a topographical context for *Bleak House*. Ironically, perhaps, the only surviving wooden house between Lincoln's Inn Fields and the Strand is now the so-called Old Curiosity Shop in Portsmouth Street. Although Dickens was insistent in the novel of that name that 'the old house had been long ago pulled down', generations have been persuaded to accept that this is the genuine article. Curious readers of *The Old Curiosity Shop* might feel gratified by this odd survival, but readers of *Bleak House* have the more eerie sensation of considering what is perhaps the last relic of Dickens's fictional slum, Tom-all-Alone's. The shift in social and architectural pretension is remarkable when we step out of Lincoln's Inn Fields and into a twisting and untidy back street. In the fields, dominated by public institutions and substantial seventeenth- and eighteenth-century brick houses, we are in orderly, airy, leafy and respectable London. In Portsmouth Street we are suddenly in what was once a far less salubrious district of narrow streets and overhanging timber buildings.

The streets stretching south-east from Portsmouth Street towards the lost Wych Street may be the imagined site of Tom-all-Alone's, the slum that Dickens was disinclined to locate precisely. His reticence on this point might seem to be anomalous given the fact that other streets and houses in the area associated with major characters are carefully placed. The chambers of the solicitors, Kenge and Carboy, are in Lincoln's Inn itself; Mr Tulkinghorn's old 'house of state' is in the fields and it has long been identified with the duly stately number 58 on the west side; Mr Snagsby, the law stationer, has a shop in the shady Cook's Court, Cursitor Street (recognizable under its disguise as the real Took's Court); Mrs Jellyby lives in the now destroyed Thavies Inn; and a property akin to Krook's rag-and-bone warehouse, in 'a narrow back street, part of some courts and lanes immediately outside the wall of the Inn', might until recent redevelopments have been identifiable. The fact that Dickens left the location of Tom-all-Alone's vague was, of course, deliberate. We know that it is near enough to the inn itself for Captain Hawdon, who lodges over Krook's warehouse, to frequent it, and for Mr Tulkinghorn to walk to it from his stately house in the fields. Tom-all-Alone's is a composite of many of London's darkest early Victorian slums; it is a 'black, dilapidated street, avoided by all decent people; where the crazy houses were seized upon, when their decay was far advanced, by some bold vagrants, who, after establishing their own possession, took to letting them out in lodgings'. Dickens's illustrator, Phiz, provided an engraved 'dark' plate showing the slum to accompany Chapter 46 of *Bleak House*. Phiz makes it look rather like Wych Street on a particularly dismal day, though the Gothic church tower he includes in his picture resembles no then existing London church. It is decidedly not the elegant Baroque steeple of St Mary-le-Strand, which can be variously seen in Henry Dixon's photographs of Wych Street, nor does it resemble the church of St Giles-in-the-Fields which once dominated the notorious St Giles's area.

Wych Street, Strand, *c.* 1870. In this wonderfully evocative photograph we are looking eastwards to the spire of St Clement Danes. All of these houses vanished in 1903. This is as near as we can get to Dickens's fictional slum of Tom-all-Alone's

Drury Lane, looking towards St Mary-le-Strand. Another haunting image from the last quarter of the nineteenth century. These seventeenth-century houses, which were demolished in 1890, may well have suggested much of Dickens's Tom-all-Alone's

Raffish though Drury Lane, Wych Street and Clare Market were in the 1850s, they had never quite descended to the social depths of the fictional Tom-all-Alone's. Clare Market was known for its cheap butchers and greengrocers and it was said to be much frequented by London's poor shopping on Saturday nights. As Dickens also noted of this area in general in *Sketches by 'Boz'*, 'The gin shops in and near Drury Lane, Holborn, St Giles's, Covent Garden and Clare Market, are the handsomest in London.' The White Lion public house in White Lion Passage had been the haunt of the notorious eighteenth-century thief Jack Wild, but by the opening years of Queen Victoria's reign the area was far from alien to 'decent people'. The Olympic Theatre, famous for the performances of Mme Vestris, stood at numbers 6–10 Wych Street. It burned to the ground in March 1849 but the premises were rebuilt so rapidly that they opened again for performances in the December of the same year and thereafter the theatre became known as a popular venue for romantic plays. Dickens's close friend

'Tom-all-Alone's'. Phiz's imaginative dark plate illustration to Chapter 46 of *Bleak House*. Dickens's slum is unlocated, but the medieval tower of the church would have had few London precedents in the 1850s

and the founder editor of *Punch*, Mark Lemon, was for a time the landlord at the Shakespeare's Head public house at number 31. Apart from the White Lion, all of these structures survived until the demolitions of 1899.

The most vile of the open sores of Tom-all-Alone's, the 'hemmed-in churchyard, pestiferous and obscene' where Captain Hawdon is so miserably interred in *Bleak House*, may well have been based on the cramped burial ground of St Mary-le-Strand in what is now Russell Street. It is long gone, but the equally cramped and hemmed-in burial yard of St Martin-in-the-Fields survives around the corner as a garden and children's playground in Drury Lane. This particular 'pestiferous' site was closed only in 1853 and was made into a garden by the St Martin's parish vestry following the Open Spaces Act of 1877, an Act which encouraged the creation of 'facilities for the enjoyment of the public of open spaces in the metropolis'. This then densely populated area must have been crying out for such facilities, even if the newly designated 'open spaces' generally had a history that was scarcely conducive to public health.

The streets off Drury Lane are still populated, though relatively few old houses survive. The area, as in the 1850s, is given its character by long-established and highly respectable theatres. The old fruit and vegetable market at Covent Garden has now gone the way of Clare Market (though its old building survives, silk scarves having generally replaced cabbage leaves). Only a very few of the modern patrons of the Royal Opera House or the Theatre Royal, Drury Lane, are likely to be aware that they are within a two-minute walk of what was, when *Bleak House* was published, 'a dreadful spot in which the very night was very slowly stirring'. When she finds her mother dead at the dripping gate of a festering graveyard Esther Summerson tells us that it was crammed with 'heaps of dishonoured graves and stones, hemmed in by filthy houses … on whose walls a thick humidity broke out like a disease'. Diverting such an account might be; entertaining it certainly would not be.

Nests of Lawyers

Only a tiny handful of latter-day visitors to the area between Drury Lane and Chancery Lane are likely to be there solely to seek out the sites of its former graveyards. If anyone should yearn for open space, however, it can readily be found in the nearby private enclaves administered by the Honourable Societies of Lincoln's Inn and the Middle and Inner Temple. On working days these enclaves are open both for business and to the orderly visitor (the less well behaved will either be visiting their lawyers or will have attracted the attention of porters and gate-keepers). There are relatively few residents in the Inns of Court nowadays, for chambers are more in demand as offices than as apartments. They were always primarily the preserve of students of the common law, of course, and readers of Dickens will particularly remember the memorable chambers occupied by

Quality Court, off Chancery Lane, c. 1900. This is a typical enough early eighteenth-century backwater in the middle of legal London. The houses were demolished in the early 1920s

Mr Vholes amid the 'congenial shabbiness' of Symond's Inn in *Bleak House* or by Mr Stryver in Paper Buildings in the Temple in *A Tale of Two Cities*. In the nineteenth century, however, it was still normal for both bachelors and young couples to rent rooms in the inns. This was as true of Tommy Traddles as it was for Charles Dickens himself (who had rooms at the now vanished Furnival's Inn).

Bleak House is rare amongst Dickens's novels in that, with the exception of the Jellyby family, so few characters seem to enjoy the conveniences of life provided in the inns. In early nineteenth-century London there were virtually no purpose-built blocks of flats or apartments. As we have seen, a Samuel Pickwick or a family of modest means like the Kenwigs in *Nicholas Nickleby* were generally content with taking sets of rooms in terraced houses where the facilities were common, and the board was provided by a resident landlady.

The Jellybys' accommodation at Thavies Inn is far more than a set of chambers, for Thavies had long since ceased to have any function as a hostel for lawyers. The Jellybys have a house which is capacious enough not only to accommodate that chaotic family but also to provide a night's accommodation for Esther, Ada and Richard. As we learn from the officious Mr Guppy in the third chapter of *Bleak House*, Thavies Inn is 'no distance' from Kenge and Carboys offices in Lincoln's Inn: 'only round the corner. We just twist up Chancery Lane, and cut along Holborn, and there we are in four minutes' time as near as a toucher.' Esther and her companions turn under an archway into 'a narrow street of high houses, like an oblong cistern to hold the fog' and find a crowd of people fretting over the fact that the youngest Jellyby child has got his head stuck in the area railings. These late eighteenth-century residences were in fact standard London brick houses occupied by 'private

Charles Dickens Museum

Thavies Inn, Holborn, *c.* 1900. This 'oblong cistern', as Dickens describes it in *Bleak House*, is the residence of the Jellyby family. Here Esther Summerson rescues the youngest Jellyby child who has his head stuck in the area railings. The Inn vanished after bomb damage in the 1940s

individuals'. The 'oblong cistern' had replaced older buildings which had burned down soon after the society was dissolved in the 1760s. What was left of the ancient Thavies Inn finally fell victim to bombs during the Second World War. It now survives only as a street name.

Younger professional men, like Dickens at the beginning of his career, were content with less spacious accommodation. He had taken a 'three pair back' in Furnival's Inn in December 1834 at a rent of £35 per annum. His three rooms facing onto an internal courtyard, plus a cellar and a lumber room, were initially to provide accommodation for Dickens and his younger brother, Frederick. When the novelist married Catherine Hogarth in April 1836 she joined her husband there, though Frederick Dickens would occasionally lodge with them, as would Catherine's sister, Mary. The rooms were, by all accounts, gloomy but large enough. Given the number of friends and relatives that the Dickenses seem to have crammed into them, they needed to be. Nevertheless, as the older novelist recalled in 1860 in his essay 'Chambers', a real distinction had to be drawn between such accommodation and that offered by a family house in London:

> It is to be remarked of chambers in general, that they must have been built for chambers, to have the right kind of loneliness. You may make a great dwelling-house very lonely by isolating suites of rooms and calling them chambers, but you cannot make the true kind of loneliness. In dwelling-houses, there have been family festivals; children have grown in them, girls have bloomed into women in them, courtships and marriages have taken place in them. True chambers were never young, childish, maidenly; never had dolls in them, or rocking-horses or christenings, or betrothals, or little coffins.

That last, singularly bleak reference to 'little coffins' reminds us of the perilous shortness of life for many Victorians. Nevertheless, what Dickens wants to say here is that the kind of chambers that were let out in the Inns of Court and the Inns of Chancery were essentially the preserve of the bachelor and the childless couple.

With children on the way, young married couples moved on from what was the equivalent of a 'first-time buy'. In *David Copperfield* this is what happens to the Traddleses, who abandon their cramped chambers in Gray's Inn for a 'large house' which is soon filled up with Traddles's wife's siblings.

The Dickenses, too, moved themselves from Furnival's Inn in 1837 to 48 Doughty Street. Having long outlasted their original function, the old buildings of Furnival's Inn on the north side of Holborn were demolished in July 1898. They were replaced by the vividly red, terracotta Gothic of Alfred Waterhouse's Prudential Assurance Building.

It is bachelors who are Dickens's most memorable occupants of chambers in the Inns of Court. Of all the inns, the Temple seems to have been the favourite. In *Great Expectations* Pip and Herbert Pocket share chambers 'at the top of the last house in Garden Court, down by the river'. This is the scene of Pip's re-encounter with Magwitch on a night of 'wretched weather' when 'a vast heavy veil' of rain has been driven over London from the east. The wild weather renders the scene 'gothic', despite the modest classicism of the actual architecture of Garden Court.

> Alterations have been made in that part of the Temple since that time, and it has not now so lonely a character as it had then, nor is it so exposed to the river. We lived at the top of the last house, and the wind rushing up the river shook the house that night, like discharges of cannon, or breakings of a sea. When the rain came with it and dashed against the windows, I thought, raising my eyes to them as they rocked, that I might have fancied myself in a storm-beaten lighthouse. Occasionally the smoke came rolling down the chimney as though it could not bear to go out on such a night, and when I set the doors open and looked down the staircase, the staircase lamps were blown out...

Garden Court is 'lonely' just as 'chambers in general' are 'lonely': it lacks the day-to-day bustle of families, children and servants. What Dickens is also telling us is that this particular area of the Middle Temple had changed its character between the 1820s, when

Fountain Court, The Temple, c. 1890. This scene is largely intact today

Garden Court was rebuilt, and the early 1860s, when work on the new Embankment would have moved the River Thames far further away from the precincts of the Temple. New buildings, including a library, had also left Garden Court far less exposed to loneliness and bad weather. It was rebuilt in 1884, and since the 1940s and war-time bomb damage, the area's architecture has again changed radically. Nevertheless, this part of the Temple remains particularly haunted by the ghosts of Dickens's characters. Nearby Fountain Court is the scene of the tryst between Ruth Pinch and John Westlock in *Martin Chuzzlewit*. The weather on this occasion is singularly more benign than that in *Great Expectations*, and Dickens waxes lyrical about the charms of this still sequestered spot:

> Brilliantly the Temple Fountain sparkled in the sun, and laughingly its liquid music played, and merrily the idle drops of water danced and danced, and peeping out in sport among the trees, plunged lightly down to hide themselves, as little Ruth and her companion came towards it ...

What a good old place it was! John said with quite an earnest affection for it.

'A pleasant place indeed,' said little Ruth. 'So shady!'....

They came to a stop when John began to praise it. The day was exquisite; and, stopping at all, it was quite natural – nothing could be more so – that they should glance down Garden Court; because Garden Court ends in the River, and that glimpse is very bright and fresh and shining on a summer's day.

The fountain in Fountain Court could not hold its head high in comparison to those of Rome. Even the present single gushing jet of water, which replaces the one familiar to Dickens, is rather a modest apology for a fountain. Nevertheless, it gives a particular distinction to what is still a quiet, out-of-the-way and relatively undiscovered place in the very centre of London. It is also one of the few places in the centre of the city to remain blessedly free of cars.

Dickens himself may well have been drawn to the Temple by its intimate associations with one of his favourite eighteenth-century writers, Oliver Goldsmith. It is in sight of Goldsmith's tomb, in the somewhat gloomy and huddled graveyard of the Temple Church, that he places the chambers occupied by Mortimer Lightwood and Eugene Wrayburn in *Our Mutual Friend*. Mortimer, who has been on 'the honourable roll of solicitors of the High Court of Chancery, and attorneys at Common Law' for five years, has his offices on the second floor of a block of chambers overlooking the churchyard. The old building was replaced by a dull, slightly fussy, but functional block, built in 1861 and named Goldsmith Buildings, but the setting is readily recognizable:

Whosoever had gone out of Fleet Street into the Temple at the date of this history, and had wandered disconsolate about the Temple until he stumbled on a dismal churchyard, and had looked up at the dismal windows commanding that churchyard until at the most dismal window of them all he saw a dismal boy, would in him have beheld, at one grand comprehensive swoop of the eye, the managing clerk, junior clerk, common-law clerk, conveyancing clerk, chancery clerk, every refinement and department of clerk, of Mr Mortimer Lightwood, erewhile called in the newspapers eminent solicitor.

Mortimer's is neither a particularly well-established firm, nor a particularly distinguished one. On the other side of the landing on the second floor, however, Dickens places the residential chambers that Mortimer shares with Eugene Wrayburn. They are obviously convenient for Mortimer's business, though, as we know his fellow resident seems to have none at all. Chapter 6 of Book Two of *Our Mutual Friend* opens as follows:

Again Mr Mortimer Lightwood and Mr Eugene Wrayburn sat together in the Temple. This evening, however, they were not together in the place of business of the eminent solicitor, but in another dismal set of chambers facing it on the same second floor; on whose dungeon-like black outer-door appeared the legend:

PRIVATE
MR EUGENE WRAYBURN
MR MORTIMER LIGHTWOOD
(*Mr Lightwood's Offices opposite*)

Appearances indicated that this establishment was a very recent institution. The white letters of the inscription were extremely white and extremely strong to the sense of smell, the complexion of the tables and chairs … a little too blooming to be believed in, and the carpets and floorcloth seemed to rush at the beholder's face in the unusual prominency of their patterns. But the Temple, accustomed to tone down both the still life and the human life that has much to do with it, would soon get the better of all that.

It is in these chambers, where the brand new furniture awkwardly waits to be dulled down by the dry usage of the Temple, that the memorably excruciating interview between Wrayburn and Bradley Headstone takes place.

Outside the same chambers, at the Temple Gate from the Strand, Bradley Headstone ominously loiters, night after night, in order to dog Eugene. Wrayburn in turn goads the schoolmaster, delighting in what he whimsically sees as 'the pleasures of the chase':

> I stroll out after dark, stroll a little way, look in at a window and furtively look out for the schoolmaster on the watch … Having made sure of his watching me, I tempt him on, all over London. One night I go east, another night north, in a few nights I go all round the compass … Thus I enjoy the pleasures of the chase, and derive great benefit from the healthful exercise. When I do not enjoy the pleasures of the chase, for anything I know he watches at the Temple Gate all night.

As we have already seen, Dickens himself was no stranger either to sleeplessness or to night walks in London. From his offices in Wellington Street, off the Strand, he must regularly have passed this same Inner Temple gateway and the alley leading past Goldsmith's Building. This was the Charles Dickens who, when he was writing *Our Mutual Friend*, was also passionately but secretly involved with the young actress Ellen Ternan. He was certainly familiar with the uneasy mind of a restless, even obsessive lover. We can but speculate, of course, but these associations seem to render the otherwise undistinguished and dingy Inner Temple Lane, the passage from Fleet Street to Temple Church, central to our experience of reading a key novel of Dickens's later years.

Prisons

Dickens was never completely at ease with himself. His unease, like the grit in an oyster, probably made him a great writer. Long before he began his restless infatuation with Ellen Ternan, he harboured secrets and scrupulously kept aspects of his past life safely hidden from public scrutiny. He may well have simply been lucky in keeping them hidden, but he also took steps to discourage both snoopers and those with an innocent interest in his background. During his lifetime, would-be biographers were given only the vaguest details of his family, his education and his early professional experience. In the summer of 1860 he engaged in a determined destruction of his correspondence in an attempt to cramp the style of any future biographer. Having burned every letter sent to him he somewhat naively assumed that his correspondents might equally destroy his letters to them. They did not, and as a consequence we now have twelve fat volumes of Dickens's collected correspondence. We also have several revealing biographies, each of which has benefited from the efforts of his first biographer, John Forster.

It was Forster's first volume, published in 1872, that revealed the traumatic nature of Dickens's boyhood and discussed both his father's bankruptcy and the humiliating year spent by the boy as a drudge at Warren's Blacking Factory at Hungerford Stairs. It may strike us as odd that, given Dickens's vast and cultivated celebrity during his lifetime, no ex-workmate at Warren's Blacking came forward to identify the famous writer as a former colleague. As far as we know they did not, and that may have been to Dickens's advantage. It certainly contributed to what Forster noted was Dickens's 'too great confidence in himself' which was coupled with 'a susceptivity almost feminine and the most eager craving for sympathy'. Dickens was as prickly about his past as he was about his secret love affair. John Forster's biography may well have revealed the secret disgrace of his childhood but it maintained an almost total silence as to the existence of Ellen Ternan.

Dickens's novels are full of prisons and, as many commentators have noted, one particular novel, *Little Dorrit*, is not only centred on a London gaol, it shows how the idea of confinement spreads like some endemic disease through all the characters. Many aspects of the book were also based on Dickens's own painful experience, though very few of its first readers would have guessed quite how personal that experience had been. In the first chapter of his biography John Forster described the effect on the young Dickens of his father's descent into debt, his arrest by court officers (at a 'sponging house') and his subsequent confinement in the Marshalsea Prison:

> The interval between the sponging-house and the prison was spent by the sorrowful lad in running errands and carrying messages for the prisoner, delivered with swollen eyes and

through shining tears; and the last words said to him by his father before he was finally carried to the Marshalsea, were to the effect that the sun was set upon him for ever. 'I really believed at the time,' said Dickens to me, 'that they had broken my heart.' He took afterwards ample revenge for this false alarm by making the world laugh at them in *David Copperfield*.

Forster almost disarms us with this last phrase. In *David Copperfield* it is David's impecunious landlord, Wilkins Micawber, who is arrested for debt and taken to the King's Bench Prison in the Borough. In Dickens's case it was his own father who was incarcerated and the prison was not only a close neighbour to the King's Bench, it was one that was to cast a very long shadow over his life and work: the Marshalsea. At the opening of Chapter 6 of *Little Dorrit*, published in 1857, he introduces us to the prison:

Thirty years ago there stood, a few doors short of the church of Saint George, in the Borough of Southwark, on the left hand side of the way going southward, the Marshalsea Prison. It had stood there many years before, and it remained there some years afterwards; but it is gone now, and the world is none the worse without it.

The Marshalsea was named for the Marshal of the King's Household who from at least the fourteenth century had confined persons supposed to have offended the royal dignity in a prison in Borough High Street. Many of them were debtors. Conditions in this delapidated structure were deemed to be so insanitary that in 1811 the prisoners were removed southwards to a new site near St George's Church. They did not, however, go to a new building but to a disused prison housed in a run-down three-storey brick block, and some additional dwellings, facing onto a yard. It is this building that Dickens describes in his second paragraph:

It was an oblong pile of barrack building, partitioned into squalid houses standing back to back, so that there were no back rooms; environed by a narrow paved yard, hemmed in by high walls duly spiked at top. Itself a close and confined prison for debtors, it contained within it a much closer and confined jail for smugglers. Offenders against the revenue laws, and defaulters to excise or customs, who had incurred fines which they were unable to pay, were supposed to be incarcerated behind an iron-plated door, closing up a second prison, consisting of a strong cell or two, and a blind alley some yard and a half wide, which formed the mysterious termination of the very limited skittle-ground in which the Marshalsea debtors bowled down their troubles.

This was therefore not much like a prison that we would recognize. As Dickens says, the debtors and the smugglers seem to have mixed freely and the governance of the whole establishment was lax and inefficient. The prisoners confined there were required to pay for what lodging they could best afford, and their victuals, fuel,

Charles Dickens Museum

The remains of the Marshalsea Prison, Borough High Street. The 'oblong pile of barrack building' described in *Little Dorrit* had been closed as a prison in 1842. What was left when Dickens revisited the site in May 1857 was an 'outer front courtyard … metamorphosed into a butter shop, adjacent to Angel Court'. 'Angel Place' survives as an alley, as does the evocative Marshalsea wall, but the buildings shown in this early twentieth-century photograph are long gone

The Marshalsea wall,
Angel Place, *c.* 1900

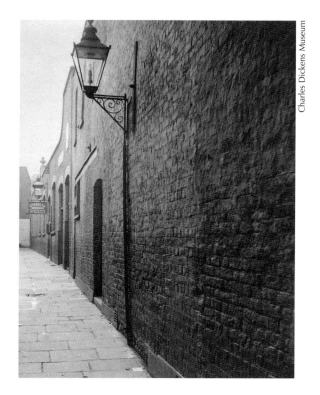

Charles Dickens Museum

furniture, bed linen and laundry had to be provided either by themselves or by their families – rather a tall order for men and women
who were at best financially 'challenged'. As we know from
Dickens's life, and from the history of William Dorrit so painfully
described in *Little Dorrit*, the families of the confined could lodge
with them in the prison if space and resources were available. These
family members could come and go, and they could find work
beyond the prison's walls; the debtors themselves had to stay put
until such time as their debts were settled or their creditors gave up
on them. It was, as *Little Dorrit* reveals, a debilitating system. The
boy Charles Dickens, who was labouring at Warren's Blacking,
lodged in Lant Street; his family were three minutes away, behind
the Marshalsea wall.

That is just about all that survives of the prison nowadays. It was
closed down in 1842 and the ground and buildings sold to an iron-
monger for the princely sum of £5,100. Some of the prison buildings

were incorporated into what became a printing works on Borough High Street. In the preface to *Little Dorrit*, which Dickens added in May 1857, he notes:

> Some of my readers may have an interest in being informed whether or no any portions of the Marshalsea Prison are yet standing. I did not know, myself, until the sixth of this present month, when I went to look. I found the outer front courtyard ... metamorphosed into a butter-shop ... Wandering ... down a certain adjacent 'Angel Court, leading to Bermondsey,' I came to 'Marshalsea Place': the houses in which I recognized, not only as the great block of the former prison, but as preserving the rooms that arose in my mind's-eye when I became Little Dorrit's biographer ... whosoever goes into Marshalsea Court, turning out of Angel Court, leading to Bermondsey, will find his feet on the very paving-stones of the extinct Marshalsea jail; will see its

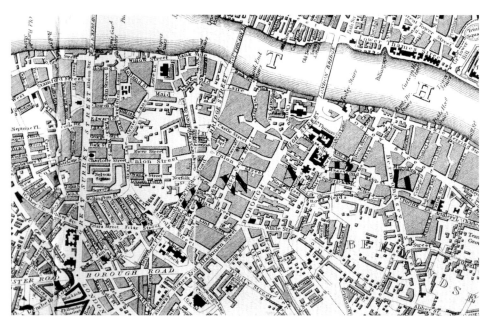

The Borough and Bermondsey, 1832. This shows the area so closely associated with Dickens's childhood

narrow yard to the right and to the left, very little altered if at all, except that the walls were lowered when the place got free; will look upon the rooms in which the debtors lived; and will stand upon the crowding ghosts of many miserable years.

There is no mention of the Dickens family being amongst those ghosts, of course.

Most of what Dickens saw in May 1857 has now gone except for the bulging brick boundary wall, bereft of its spikes. One side of this wall borders an alley now named Angel Place; on the other side of it lies the former graveyard of St George's Church. Here in the graveyard, now a scrubby little park bravely renamed 'St George's Gardens', we get our best view of one of the most evocative Dickensian sites. Whether it is a drizzly winter's day, a sunny August afternoon or an evening when the long shadows play on the bricks, it might seem to some to be a commonplace object of pilgrimage, but that does not render this fragment of a wailing wall any less haunting. For readers of Dickens, 'the crowding ghosts' are still there.

The English Law made its presence felt in the Borough in two other prisons, both of which have their impact on Dickens's life and fiction. The King's Bench Prison once stood on a site a little south of the Marshalsea, on the corner of Borough Road and Borough High Street. This area was once known as Stones End. Part of the prison had been torched by the Gordon Rioters in 1780 (a fact referred to briefly in *Barnaby Rudge*) and another section burned in 1799 (probably as a result of an accident). The restored structure that Dickens knew was described by an anonymous writer in 1823 as 'a good and substantial brick building, containing eight spacious and excellent apartments let at one shilling a week, to the oldest prisoners, or those who, by their good conduct and gentlemanly behaviour, have entitled themselves to this indulgence'. The prison also boasted reading rooms, a fives court, a surgery, a taproom, a public kitchen and bakehouse and up to thirty gin shops. Debtors imprisoned in the King's Bench were, on the payment of a fee of 5 guineas (for small debts) or 8 guineas (for larger debts), allowed out on parole in an area known as the Rules, which extended out from the Borough into the open land known as St George's Fields. It is in a row of 'mean and not over-cleanly houses' within the Rules that Walter Bray and his daughter, Madeline, live in *Nicholas Nickleby*.

> The Rules are a certain liberty adjoining the prison, and comprising some dozen streets in which debtors who can raise money to pay large fees, from which their creditors do *not* derive any benefit, are permitted to reside by the wise provisions of the same enlightened laws which leave the debtor who can raise no money to starve in jail, without the food, clothing, lodging or warmth, which are provided for felons convicted of the most atrocious crimes that can disgrace humanity.

Such was the extent of the Rules that Nicholas only finds the row of houses where the Brays live 'after traversing a very dirty and dusty suburb, of which minor theatricals, shell-fish, ginger-beer, spring vans, green-grocery, and brokers' shops appeared to compose the main and most prominent features'.

It is within the spiked walls of the King's Bench Prison itself, however, that David Copperfield visits Mr Micawber for a 'gypsy-like' dinner on his first Sunday as an enforced resident there. Micawber, unlike Walter Bray, can neither afford to live within the Rules nor support the genteel lifestyle to which he aspires, even in a debtors' prison:

> Mr Micawber was waiting for me within the gate, and we went up to his room (top storey but one), and cried very much ... After which he borrowed a shilling of me for porter, gave me a written order on Mrs Micawber for the amount, and put away his pocket-handkerchief, and cheered up.
>
> We sat before a little fire, with two bricks put within the rusted grate, to prevent its burning too many coals; until another debtor, who shared the room with Mr Micawber, came in from the bake-house with the loin of mutton which was our joint-stock repast. Then I was sent up to 'Captain Hopkins' in the room overhead, with Mr Micawber's compliments, and I was his young friend, and would Captain Hopkins lend me a knife and fork.

Captain Hopkins, who is described as being 'in the last extremity of shabbiness', lives in the room with a 'very dirty lady' (who is evidently not Mrs Hopkins), and two 'wan' girls (his daughters). Dickens may well have been remembering one of his father's neighbours in the Marshalsea.

When the Fleet Prison and the Marshalsea were closed by Act of Parliament in 1842, the King's Bench (by now the Queen's Bench) became London's sole prison for debtors and bankrupts. At this time, both the Rules and all other fees and special privileges were abolished. Imprisonment for debt was itself abolished in 1869 and what was now called the Queen's Prison was closed. Its site was sold by auction in 1879 and the buildings were demolished in the following year. Nothing now marks its somewhat unhappy, but eccentric, existence.

On the other side of Borough High Street is an innocuous-looking street now known as Harper Road. This is the third name that this street has borne. It was formerly Union Road, and was entered from Borough High Street by a narrow passage called Horsemonger Lane. It had a dark reputation in Dickens's day as the site of the Surrey County Gaol, commonly known as the Horsemonger Lane Gaol. All that remains to remind us of its Victorian associations is the handsome neo-Baroque Court House on the corner of Newington Causeway. This stands on the site of the Sessions House attached to the gaol. The old court building was demolished in 1912, having outlived the old Horsemonger Lane Gaol by some thirty-four years. The prison building dated from the closing years of the eighteenth century and consisted of a three-storey quadrangle. It had briefly enjoyed celebrity status in 1812–14 when Leigh Hunt had been confined there for a libel against the Prince Regent, and had been visited by Lord Byron and Thomas Moore. In 1862 Henry Mayhew described the building as 'enclosed within a dingy brick wall', but he also noted its only noteworthy architectural feature, a rusticated gatehouse decorated with carved balls and chains:

We enter the gateway of the flat-roofed building at the entrance to the prison, on one side of which is the governor's office, and an apartment occupied by the gate-warder, and on the other is a staircase leading up to a gloomy chamber, containing the scaffold on which many a wretched criminal has been consigned to public execution.

It was the flat-roofed gatehouse that generally attracted public notice, for here ghoulish crowds gathered to watch public hangings.

The most notorious of these public executions attracted some 30,000 spectators. Charles Dickens was amongst the vast crowd that assembled on the morning of 13 November 1849 to witness the judicial end of Frederick George Manning and his Swiss-born wife, Maria. The Mannings, who had been held in the gaol, and tried at the Old Bailey, had been found guilty of the murder of a former lover of Maria's, a money-lender called Patrick O'Connor, whose body had been found, covered in quicklime, under the kitchen floor of the Mannings' house in Bermondsey. He had been shot in the head and then bludgeoned with a blunt instrument. When arrested by the police, Frederick Manning had claimed that it was Maria who had instigated the crime and who had actually shot O'Connor (though he admitted to finishing him off with a crowbar). What shocked many middle-class Victorians was that a woman could have committed such a terrible crime and had then attempted to exploit a series of legal loopholes in order to avoid conviction. This was seen as an example of un-English and un-feminine wickedness. It is very probable that Maria's brazenness contributed to Dickens's portrait of the fiery Hortense, the murderous French maid in *Bleak House* (Maria too had served as a lady's maid).

The Mannings certainly fascinated Dickens the novelist, but Dickens the social commentator was drawn to the scene of their execution to observe the crowd rather than the victims. Rooms in the tenements opposite the gaol had been let out to more affluent spectators (including Dickens, who had paid 10 guineas for a good view), but a rather more vicious but equally curious body of poorer men and women jostled one another in the street below. Pick-pocketing, swearing and personal abuse appear to have been rife. Dickens went to Horsemonger Lane at intervals during the night before and remained there continuously from daybreak 'until after the spectacle was over'. His shock at the demeanour, behaviour and responses of the crowd stimulated him to write two considered letters of protest to *The Times*. Both were reprinted as handbills and distributed to the general public.

> I believe that a sight so inconceivably awful as the wickedness and levity of the immense crowd collected at that execution this morning could be imagined by no man, and could be presented in no heathen land under the sun. The horrors of the gibbet and of the crime which brought the wretched murderers to it, faded in my mind before the atrocious bearing, looks and language, of the assembled spectators. When I came upon the scene at midnight, the *shrillness* of the cries and howls that were raised from time to time, denoting that they came from a concourse of boys and girls already assembled in the best places made my blood run cold ... When the sun rose brightly ... it gilded thousands upon thousands of upturned faces, so inexpressibly odious in their brutal mirth or callousness, that a man had cause to feel ashamed of the shape he wore, and to shrink from himself, as fashioned in the image of the Devil. When the two miserable creatures who attracted all this ghastly sight about them, were turned quivering in the air, there was no more emotion, no more pity, no more thought that two immortal souls had gone to judgment, no more restraint in any of the previous obscenities, than if the name of Christ had never been heard in this world, and there were no belief among men but that they perished like the beasts.

As Dickens insisted, he did not believe that any community could prosper 'where such a scene of horror and demoralization ... is passed by, unknown and forgotten'. He was not to waver in his opposition to public hangings, though the barbarous practice was not stopped for another twenty years.

As time passed Dickens found it difficult to dismiss memories of the Mannings' execution from his mind. He was to recall it with a shiver of nocturnal horror in the revealing essay 'Lying Awake' which he published in his journal *Household Words* in October

1852. During a sleepless night he remembers not just the 'dismal spectacle' of the Mannings, 'husband and wife, hanging on the top of Horsemonger Lane Jail', but also his compulsive returns to the spot during his habitual perambulations of the streets of London.

> Having beheld that execution, and having left those two forms dangling on the top of the entrance gateway – the man's, a limp loose suit of clothes, as if the man had gone out of them; the woman's, a fine shape, so elaborately corseted and artfully dressed that it was quite unchanged in its trim appearance as it slowly swung from side to side – I never could, by my utmost efforts, for some weeks, present the outside of that prison to myself ... without presenting it with the two figures still hanging in the morning air. Until, strolling past the gloomy place one night, when the street was deserted and quiet, and actually seeing that the bodies were not there, my fancy was persuaded, as it were, to take them down and bury them within the precincts of the jail, where they have lain ever since.

This is vivid writing, and it gives us a clue to how the darker side of Dickens's imagination worked.

As was customary, the Mannings had been buried inside Horsemonger Lane Gaol. When the prison was closed in August 1878 and demolished two years later their grave markers were preserved and are now displayed in the Borough of Southwark's Cuming Museum in the Walworth Road. Somewhat incongruously, in 1884 Mrs Gladstone, the wife of the Prime Minister, opened a children's playground on the site of the prison. It is now a small park called Newington Gardens. Dickens might well have felt that this was a way of erasing painful memories.

At the time, very few people regretted the passing of Southwark's three Dickensian prisons. Despite their associations, none was at all distinguished architecturally. Though even fewer people mourned the actual closure of London's most notorious prison, Newgate, in 1902 a body of concerned conservationists did fight for the preservation of its monumental façade. In the event, the only part of the structure that was conserved was the old condemned cell, which was rebuilt in the cellars of Lancaster House in the Mall, which then housed the Museum of London; the cell door and other relics are now in the new museum. Newgate Prison had been rebuilt in its final form between 1770 and 1778 to the designs of the architect George Dance. At the centre of its Old Bailey façade was the five-bay, four-storey governor's house, the only section of the outer part of the prison with windows. The rest of the great, heavily rusticated curtain wall, stretching from the Old Bailey round into Newgate Street, was windowless. The façade was relieved and animated by six hefty niches, the style of which reminded many informed commentators of the celebrated Piranesi etchings of fantastic prisons (the *Carceri d'Invenzione*). Despite its dire reputation and the sheer nastiness of life within its walls, the exterior of Newgate Prison was always much admired as a grand enhancement of London's street architecture. One critic described it, after its demolition, as 'one of the finest monumental structures London has ever seen'.

We have already noted the importance of Newgate Prison to Dickens, and something of the role it plays in his fiction. Here we

Newgate Prison, 1914. The great Prison shown just before its demolition. The central bay was the Governor's House. The open space in front of the Prison was the site of public executions

The Governor's House, Newgate Prison, 1914. The only part of the Prison with windows looking onto the street

can look at how he used the adjacent court house, popularly known as the Old Bailey. This is properly the name of a once narrow street running between Newgate and Ludgate Hill. Here stood London's pillory, last used in June 1830, and outside the prison scaffolds had been regularly erected from December 1783 (when public executions were moved here from Tyburn) to May 1868 (when the last public hanging took place). The Old Bailey Sessions House, which Dickens knew, was a building of 1778. It and the neighbouring prison were burned out by the Gordon Rioters in 1780 but both were rapidly restored to active use. This old building survived until 1902. When Newgate Prison was knocked down, the courts were lavishly rebuilt on what had been the extensive site of the gaol. The present structure, officially called the Central Criminal Court, was opened by King Edward VII in 1907. Dickens described cases being heard in the two old court rooms in 1834, in one of his early *Sketches by 'Boz'*: 'Nothing is so likely to strike the person who enters them for the first time, as the calm indifference with which the proceedings are conducted; every trial seems a mere matter of business. There is a great deal of form, but no compassion.'

Sessions were held eight times a year. In one of the courts Charles Darnay would have been tried for high treason in *A Tale of Two Cities*, though his must have been one of the last trials held there before the conflagration caused by the Gordon rioters. In the reconstructed courts Fagin would have been condemned to death in *Oliver Twist* and Magwitch tried in *Great Expectations*. In the latter novel Pip movingly recalls the proceedings when, on the last day of the Sessions, Magwitch is sentenced to death with thirty-two other convicted felons.

> The whole scene starts out again in the vivid colours of the moment, down to the drops of April rain on the windows of the court, glittering in the rays of April sun. Penned in the dock, as I again stood outside it at the corner with his hand in mine, were the two-and-thirty men and women: some defiant, some stricken with terror, some sobbing and weeping, some covering their faces, some staring gloomily about. There had been shrieks from among the women convicts, but they had been stilled and a hush had succeeded … The sun was striking in at the great windows of the court, through the glittering drops of rain upon the glass, and it made a broad shaft of light between the two-and-thirty and the Judge, linking both together, and perhaps reminding some among the audience, how both were passing on, with absolute equality, to the greater Judgment that knoweth all things and cannot err.

Again, there is a great deal of form, but scant evidence of official compassion. On receiving his death sentence, Magwitch tells the judge: 'My Lord, I have received my sentence of Death from the Almighty; but I bow to yours.' He escapes execution by dying in prison of the injuries he sustained in his desperate last struggle with his nemesis, Compeyson.

Charles Darnay also escapes execution in *A Tale of Two Cities*, but in his case his potential manner of judicial death was infinitely more horrible. The novel is set in the last decades of the eighteenth century, when English law still threatened convicted traitors with hanging, drawing and quartering. Dickens probably based Darnay's trial on that of the Baron de la Motte, a French nobleman resident in England who was found guilty of treason in July 1781. His sentence was, to quote the *Annual Register*, 'to be hanged by the neck, but not till dead; then to be cut down, and his bowels taken out and burnt before his face, his head to be taken off, his body cut into four quarters, and to be at his majesty's disposal'. The prospect of this punishment even strikes the hardened body-snatcher Jerry Cruncher as 'barbarous' (though, of course, mutilated bodies would have been of little interest to him). What is more, had Darnay been found guilty his sentence would have been carried out, not in front of Newgate Prison, but at Tyburn. That would have meant his being dragged on a hurdle from the prison through the muddy streets at Holborn Hill, along Holborn itself, through an inconvenient dog-leg of lanes near St Giles's Church and then along the length of Oxford Street to the gallows at what is now Marble Arch. This journey, which was intended to offer a series of last unpleasant humiliations to the prisoner, was merely the prelude to the slow and bloody agony of death by hanging, drawing and quartering. Dickens and his readers would have shuddered at the horror of the 'justice' meted out by their grandparents. As the novelist cynically noted on England in the 1780s: 'Altogether, the Old Bailey, at that date, was a choice illustration of the precept "Whatever is is right;" an aphorism that would be as final as it is lazy, did it not include the troublesome consequence, that nothing that ever was, was wrong.'

Dickens recognized that much remained wrong with the England of his own times. As we have seen, he also identified many of the ills that beset the kingdom and its capital as stemming from a befuddled and often unwieldy legal system. It was not just a matter of death sentences, public hangings, unfeeling judges, do-nothing attorneys, red-tape, official inertia and ramshackle prisons. To Dickens, the entanglements of the law seemed to trip up many more people than the law supported. Those men and women who tripped fell into the hands of lawyers who made a living out of entangling things further. In *David Copperfield* that quintessential professional man of law, Mr Spenlow, explains to the hero why nothing in the legal system ought to be changed:

> I asked Mr Spenlow what he considered the best sort of profes-
> sional business? He replied, that a good case of a disputed will,
> where there was a neat little estate of thirty or forty thousand
> pounds, was, perhaps the best of all. In such a case, he said, not
> only were there very pretty pickings, in the way of arguments at
> every stage of the proceedings, and mountains upon mountains of
> evidence on interrogatory and counter-interrogatory (to say
> nothing of an appeal lying, first to the Delegates, and then to the
> Lords); but, the costs being pretty sure to come out of the estate
> at last, both sides went at it in a lively and spirited manner, and
> expense was no consideration.

Mr Spenlow's glee in defining the niceties of his profession seems to descend into a kind of legal gobbledegook. The lawyer's delight, in Dickens's eyes, was the litigant's despair. This would become the central theme of *Bleak House*. In that novel the case of *Jarndyce* v. *Jarndyce* has dragged on so long that it has become a standing joke to the legal profession. That, Dickens wryly remarks, was 'the only good that had ever come out of it'. Articled clerks, we are told, have been in the habit of fleshing their legal wit upon it, and even the most elevated of lawmen attempt dry quips based upon its eternal convolutions: 'The last Lord Chancellor handled it neatly when, correcting Mr Blowers, the eminent silk gown, who said that such a thing might happen when the sky rained potatoes, he observed, 'or when we get through Jarndyce and Jarndyce, Mr Blowers'; – a pleasantry that particularly tickled the maces, bags and purses.' What many modern readers miss is the joke implicit in the very name 'Jarndyce', an older pronunciation of the name of the disease commonly called jaundice. The name is derived from the French word *jaune*. This morbid condition, caused by an obstruction of the bile, turns the whites of a sufferer's eyes yellow and adds a sickly yellowish tint to the skin. It is an appropriate metaphor in *Bleak House*, suggesting as it does both obstruction within the body politic and the yellowness of the pervasive London fog. This is all beyond a joke. Thanks to the law's obfuscations London is clogged up and increasingly unable to function properly. Given the evidence of his novels, it should not really surprise us that Charles Dickens was so *jaundiced* about the law's delays.

CHAPTER FOUR

Dickens and the Outer Suburbs: From Barnet to Greenwich

E VERY SO OFTEN Charles Dickens adopts the tone of a provocative philistine. Take for example the account of his approach to the Eternal City, Rome, in his *Pictures from Italy*. He and his party had travelled through the undulating dreariness of the Campagna, along the ancient Via Flaminia, before approaching the hills just to the north of the city.

> When we were fairly going off again, we began, in a perfect fever, to strain our eyes for Rome; and when, after another mile or two, the Eternal City appeared, at length, in the distance; it looked like – I am half afraid to write the word – like LONDON!!! There it lay, under a thick cloud, with innumerable towers, and steeples, and roofs of houses, rising into the sky, and high above them all, one Dome. I swear, that keenly as I felt the seeming absurdity of the comparison, it was so like London, at that distance, that if you could have shown it me in a glass, I should have taken it for nothing else.

It is absurd, of course, and Dickens knows it. What he wants to do is to deflate pretension and to undo the expressions of breathless wonder so common amongst first-time visitors to Italy. Dickens is determined to show no trace of what is often called the Stendhal syndrome, which renders swooning tourists incapacitated when confronted with the glories of Italian art. For him, the first glimpse of Rome and of the dome of St Peter's is neither overwhelming nor anti-climactic. It is simply, and uncannily, reminiscent of London.

As we have seen, from his youth up, Dickens had been delighted by the prospect of 'the cupola of St Paul's looming through the smoke'. It was the cityscape that was normative to him, and by it he tended to judge all other cities. He liked cities that were neither too contained nor too ordered. Above all, he liked bustle and crowds, and human and architectural variety. Given these prejudices, it is not really surprising that he generally seems to have liked Rome, but he rapidly discovered that it was a city very unlike London. The Rome of the 1840s was a walled city. It still is, but it now sprawls far beyond these ancient defences. The papal Rome of the 1840s fitted very easily within its walls, but essentially it only fitted into the north-western third of the area they enclosed. Elsewhere, there were spectacular ruins and scrubby remains, palaces and market gardens, basilicas, monasteries and the occasional villa, all set in relatively open land. To some undiscriminating visitors it must have seemed like a slightly run-down theme park. Nobody could really have mistaken it for early Victorian London.

When Dickens made his comparison of the distant prospects of Rome and London he did it very self-consciously. He may also have been making a reference to contemporary art. He probably knew, for example, Sir Charles Eastlake's once celebrated painting *Italian Scene in the Anno Santo: Pilgrims Arriving in Sight of Rome and St Peter's: Evening* (1827) which shows a group of colourfully dressed peasant pilgrims lost either in prayer or in awe at the prospect of the Holy City before them. Readers of *Pictures from Italy* probably also guessed why he made the comparison if they knew the famous views of London from Hampstead Heath which had been painted by John Constable. On a somewhat less elevated level, they may also have remembered a vignette illustration to Dickens's novel *The Old Curiosity Shop*, which showed Little Nell and her grandfather looking down on smoky London from one of the northern heights, resting and picnicking as they make their escape. The same scene was the subject of the young William Holman Hunt's painting *Little Nell and her Grandfather*, which was exhibited at the British Institution in 1846.

Dickens meticulously describes the couple's journey out of London. They leave the Old Curiosity Shop in the first hours of daylight and pass through 'the labyrinth of men's abodes which … lay between them and the outskirts'. They take by-ways rather than highways, avoiding 'the haunts of commerce', until they reach a 'straggling neighbourhood' of 'poor streets where faded gentility essayed with scanty space and shipwrecked means to make its last, feeble stand'. Finally, past brick fields, gardens, nettles and 'oyster shells, heaped in rank confusion', the built-up inner suburbs begin to melt into the half-built streets of downmarket villa-land.

At length these streets, becoming more straggling yet, dwindled and dwindled, until there were only small garden patches bordering the road, with many a summer-house innocent of paint and built of old timber or some fragments of a boat, green as the tough cabbage-stalks that grew about it, and grottoed at the seams with toad-stools and tight-sticking snails. To these succeeded pert cottages, two and two with plots of ground in front, laid out in angular beds with stiff box borders and narrow paths between, where foot-step never strayed to make the gravel rough. Then came the public-house, freshly-painted in green and white, with tea-gardens and a bowling green, spurning its old neighbour with the horse-trough where the waggons stopped; then fields; then some houses, one by one, of goodly size with lawns, some even with a lodge where dwelt a porter and his wife. Then came a turnpike; then fields again with trees and haystacks; then a hill; and on top of that the traveller might stop, and – looking back at old Saint Paul's looming through the smoke, its cross peeping above the cloud (if the day were clear) and glittering in the sun; and casting his eyes upon the Babel out of which it grew until he traced it down to the furthest outposts of the invading army of bricks and mortar whose station lay for the present nearly at his feet – might feel at last that he was clear of London.

This is an unrivalled account of the 'straggling' outer limits of London in the 1840s and, though generalized, it is based on very close observation. Here we have the shanties and the run-down survivals of lost gentility succeeded by the kind of countryside that Dickens must commonly have noted in his long walks and occasional rides into still rural Middlesex. His companions on these excursions in the late 1830s and early 1840s were John Forster and the novelist William Harrison Ainsworth. Ainsworth's biographer describes the now lost charms of Middlesex that they encountered as they rode out from Ainsworth's convivial house at Kensal Lodge:

> The three *literati* would gallop off for miles into the lovely country that stretched away to the north and west. Away by Twyford Abbey and the clear, winding Brent to tiny Perivale and Greenford, most sylvan of hamlets, through the green vale of Middlesex to Ruislip, and home by Stanmore and Harrow; or another day, away across breezy Old Oak Common to Acton, stopping for a few minutes at Berrymead Priory to exchange greetings with Bulwer-Lytton, on through Acton's narrow High Street, with its quaint, raised pavement and ancient red-tiled houses ... past Ealing's parks and long village green, round through orchard-bordered lanes to Chiswick ... and so by Shepherd's Bush to Wood Lane and the Scrubs, home again.

A 'delightful country', this nostalgic writer adds. As 'country' it is all long gone. To most modern Londoners the rural names he so lovingly recounts now recall underground stations on the Central and Piccadilly Lines or a long drag westwards on the motorway to Heathrow.

None of these routes westward were the weary road trod by Little Nell and her grandfather. We cannot really be sure on precisely which hill they paused for their picnic. Properly, they should have followed the road out of London towards Highgate, and it was on Highgate Hill that Holman Hunt chose to paint them in 1846. It is equally possible, however, that they might have taken a less steep route through Hampstead or followed the Edgware Road towards Hendon. It does not really signify. What does signify in *The Old Curiosity Shop* is that its most important characters seek to get *out* of London rather than *into* it. This is a rather unusual direction in

Dickens's novels. He even refers to London as 'Babel' before shifting from a biblical metaphor to a Bunyanesque one. On looking down on London from the northern heights, Nell recalls the old copy of *Pilgrim's Progress* 'with strange plates' that had sat on a shelf in the Curiosity Shop:

> As she looked back upon the place they had left, one part of it came strongly on her mind.
>
> 'Dear Grandfather,' she said, 'only that this place is prettier and a great deal better than the real one, if that in the book is like it, I feel as if we were both Christian, and laid down on this grass all the cares and troubles we brought with us; never to take them up again.'

Her grandfather insists that they will 'never ... return'. Dickens therefore sees the pair as happily leaving the City of Destruction and freeing themselves from the taints and blights of the sinful city. They are now seeking salvation well beyond its limits. Dickens does not usually feel inclined to show us London in such a bad light.

Nevertheless, the imaginative description of the outer suburbs through which Nell and her grandfather have passed does reveal something of Dickens's deepseated understanding of the invigorating nature of the metropolis. Little Nell wants nothing further to do with London, but Dickens's observant description of the Middlesex highways of the early 1840s suggests that he was well aware that the fields and market gardens and the suburban villas were integrally linked to the future of London. Essentially, they were already in London's thrall. By the end of Dickens's life most of the Middlesex fields through which Nell and her grandfather trudged had been built over. The pastures and the gardens of the larger villas had been developed as residential estates, the villages were swamped by new commercial properties and the countryside had retreated further northwards and westwards. What had been unadulterated agricultural land in the 1840s had already been turned into the kind of half-finished, straggling suburbia described in *The Old Curiosity Shop*.

The seemingly inexorable process of the development and rede-

velopment of the Home Counties was only curtailed by the introduction of the Green Belt in the 1930s. Built-up London was halted
in its tracks at Barnet and Mill Hill, at Esher and Orpington. It was
then obliged to jump over green land before reasserting its semi-
urban identity (albeit with a distinctly *suburban* accent). After the
introduction of the Green Belt the outermost suburbs began to be
populated by rich Londoners who liked to pretend that they were
not Londoners at all.

Straggling London: Camden Town, Holloway and Walworth

Readers of Dickens's novels have to remember that the London he
describes was much more limited in its sprawl than it became in the
second half of the nineteenth century and the first third of the
twentieth. It was still a place that was quite easy to get out of, as
some of his characters happily experience. Take, for example,
Esther Summerson's account of the journey out of foggy Thavies
Inn in Holborn towards St Albans in *Bleak House*:

> The day had brightened very much, and still brightened as we
> went westward. We went our way through the sunshine and the
> fresh air, wondering more and more at the extent of the streets,
> the brilliancy of the shops, the great traffic, and the crowds of
> people whom the pleasanter weather seemed to have brought out
> like many-coloured flowers. By-and-bye we began to leave the
> wonderful city, and to proceed through suburbs which, of them-
> selves, would have made a pretty large town, in my eyes; and at
> last we got into real country road again, with windmills, rick-
> yards, milestones, farmers' waggons, scents of old hay, swinging
> signs and horse troughs: trees, fields, and hedgerows. It was
> delightful to see the green landscape before us, and the immense
> metropolis behind.

Rather than feeling as if they have thrown off the burden of the
city's sins, Esther and her companions seem to understand that

London and London's countryside actually complement one another. Richard Carstone is even prompted to proclaim that the whole road has reminded him of Dick Whittington, though he does not suggest that they turn back to London in order to make their fortunes. That mention of Dick Whittington, the semi-legendary poor-country-boy-made-good-in-London, does, however, remind readers that London is not just another incarnation of Babel or the true name of the City of Destruction: it is a place of opportunity and personal fulfilment. Confusing and dirty Esther Summerson may have found the inner city, but her language tells us that she finds it exhilarating.

During Dickens's lifetime, however, many working Londoners had resolved not to live in the heavily urbanized and smoky centre but in what were then deemed to be its more breezy outer suburbs. They were not always prosperous Londoners. The advent of the railway was to facilitate daily journeyings to and fro, and bricky London accordingly expanded outwards in every direction. The 1840s also marked the dawning of the age of the commuter. As we have already noted, Dickens's London is essentially a pedestrian's city and Dickens's most distinctive commuters travel from their suburbs to work by foot. These tend to be lower middle-class Londoners. Bob Cratchit in A Christmas Carol daily retraces much of the boy Dickens's route into central London from his house in Camden Town.

Camden Town had begun to be laid out by the Earl of Camden in the last years of the eighteenth century, but it was not any grand scheme. The area sufficed with a simple grid layout and the kind of resident who never aspired to fashion. By the time the Dickens family rented their small terraced house in Bayham Street in 1823 it had a distinct air of being 'faded'. In Chapter 17 of David Copperfield the narrator goes to visit Tommy Traddles, who lodges in a very similar house to that rented by the Dickenses:

> He lived in a little street near the Veterinary College at Camden Town, which was principally tenanted, as one of our clerks who lived in that direction informed me, by gentleman students, who bought live donkeys and made experiments on those quadrupeds

Bayham Street, Camden Town. This row of lower-middle-class terraced houses, dating from the early 1820s, was demolished in 1910

in their private apartments … I found that the street was not as desirable a one as I could have wished it to be, for the sake of Traddles. The inhabitants appeared to have a propensity to throw any little trifles they were not in want of, into the road: which not only made it rank and sloppy, but untidy too, on account of the cabbage-leaves. The refuse was not wholly vegetable either, for I myself saw a shoe, a doubled-up saucepan, a black bonnet, and an umbrella, in various stages of decomposition, as I was looking out for the number I wanted.

An equally unflattering picture of Camden Town is given in *Dombey and Son*, though here part of the area had already begun to change due to the destructive incursions of the new railway into Euston. In the novel the Toodle family live in a particularly 'straggly' part of Camden Town, 'a little row of houses, with little squalid patches of ground before them' called Staggs's Garden (so named, we assume, because it had been developed as a speculation: a 'stag' is one who sells a new issue of shares immediately on purchase in order to make a quick profit). The neighbourhood, like the Toodles themselves, is as yet 'shy to own the Railroad':

> One or two bold speculators had projected streets; and one had built a little, but had stopped among the mud and ashes to consider farther of it ... There were frowzy fields, and cow-houses, and dunghills, and dustheaps, and ditches, and gardens and summer-houses, and carpet-beating grounds, at the very door of the Railway. Little tumuli of oyster shells in the oyster season, and of lobster shells in the lobster season, and of broken crockery, and faded cabbage leaves in all seasons, encroached upon its high places. Posts and rails, and old cautions to trespassers, and backs of mean houses and patches of wretched vegetation stared it out of countenance ... If the miserable waste ground lying near it could have laughed, it would have laughed it to scorn, like many of the miserable neighbours.

We know from *Pickwick Papers* that oysters and poverty were assumed to go together, but so it seems did the ubiquitous cabbage leaves. Nevertheless, Staggs's Gardens was 'regarded by its population as a sacred grove not to be withered by railroads'. As we have already seen, however, the railway was on the point of sweeping it, and slovenly suburbs like it, away for ever.

Lest we assume that the blight of a suburb like the unlovely Staggs's Gardens was due solely to the potential disruption of a new railway we should remember Dickens's account of two further partly developed areas on the fringes of built-up London. In *Our Mutual Friend* another pedestrian commuter into the city, Reginald Wilfer, has a house at Holloway to the north east of what we now call King's Cross.

> His home was in the Holloway region north of London, and then divided from it by fields and trees. Between Battle Bridge and that part of the Holloway district in which he dwelt, was a tract of suburban Sahara, where tiles and bricks were burnt, bones were boiled, carpets were beat, rubbish was shot, dogs were fought, and dust was heaped by contractors. Skirting the border of this desert,

by the way he took, when the light of its kiln-fires made lurid smears on the fog, R. Wilfer sighed and shook his head.

'Ah me!' said he, 'what might have been is not what is.'

R. Wilfer, who is hen-pecked by his niggling wife, is referring to his domestic arrangement, not to the area in which he lives. Their house is obviously commodious enough not only to hold the Wilfer family, but also to offer accommodation to a lodger. Both R. W. and the lodger will continue to 'skirt the border' of this suburban desert on the way to their respective places of employment.

South of the River Thames, in Walworth, lives Mr Wemmick in *Great Expectations*. The part of Walworth furthest away from town had been described by Dickens in 'The Black Veil', one of the *Sketches by 'Boz'* published in 1836, as 'a straggling, miserable place' which contained 'very many houses … sprinkled about at irregular intervals … of the rudest and most miserable description'. This unflattering comment is capped with the observation that even this was an improvement on Walworth's condition at the beginning of the century when it had been 'little better than a dreary waste, inhabited by a few scattered people of questionable character'. We cannot be absolutely certain when Wemmick is supposed to be living at Walworth but he seems to be quite at home in his unlovely, untidy, unplanned and unpretentious suburb. His pretensions are reflected in the pride he takes in his whimsical 'castle'. When Pip and he arrive at Walworth from Little Britain Pip appears to be a little taken aback:

> It appeared to be a collection of back lanes, ditches, and little gardens, and to present the aspect of a rather dull retirement. Wemmick's house was a little wooden cottage in the midst of plots of garden, and the top of it was cut out and painted like a battery mounted with guns.
> 'My own doing,' said Wemmick. 'Looks pretty don't it?'
> I highly commended it. I think it was the smallest house I ever saw; with the queerest gothic windows (by far the greater part of them sham), and a gothic door, almost too small to get in at.

At the back of this island estate live a pig, fowls and rabbits. It also boasts a cucumber frame and a bower 'about a dozen yards off, but which was approached by such ingenious twists of paths that it took quite a long time to get at'.

Wemmick's commuter mentality, with its strict division between work (Little Britain) and domestic life (Walworth), may strike many modern readers as familiar enough. What they might find singularly *un*familiar is the architecture and setting of the 'castle'. Uniformity, imposed by developers, planners and planning laws, now reigns in the suburbs. Latter-day Wemmicks may retain their whimsy, but few men like him would dare to affront neighbours, who are very likely to be wedded to respectable conformity, with such eccentric tastes in architecture. Neither R. Wilfer's Holloway nor Wemmick's Walworth are remotely recognizable today. The only places in modern Britain where we can glimpse such determined whimsy is in certain well-established communities of working-class retirees at the seaside. As far as I have observed, the only areas which immediately recall Dickens's descriptions of these long-lost suburbs are now in the Netherlands and north-eastern France. On the fringes of Dutch and French cities allotments have been set aside by canals, rivers and railways where on weekend evenings older men and women sit on the verandahs of their little wooden summer houses and smoke contentedly while they admire the plump vegetables in their cucumber frames. There are, however, no conspicuous tumuli of oyster shells.

Excelsior! The Northern Heights of London

Anyone looking at a map of late eighteenth-century or early nineteenth-century London will realize that the city expanded outwards along the lines of its main roads. Like some gigantic organism, London initially sent out tendrils and, having allowed them to establish firm roots, it then colonized the surrounding areas. First came the late Georgian brick terraces of houses along the main arteries leading out of London, then villas, neatly laid out behind them in squares, groves, closes and crescents, then finally the speculative estates arrived. This process can still be readily recognized along Upper Street and Holloway Road in Islington, along Kingsland Road, Stoke Newington Road and Green Lanes in Hackney, along the King's Road and Fulham Road in Chelsea, along Kennington Road, Brixton Road and Clapham Road in Lambeth and along the Old Kent Road in Southwark. It was all unplanned and was largely the outcome of private speculation. The rumble of traffic seems to have been no deterrent to the well-off people who first moved into these terraced houses. They remained just about 'respectable' houses until well into the nineteenth century. In one of Dickens's *Christmas Stories* of 1852, 'The Poor Relation's Story', the 'poor relation' himself lives on the Clapham Road in 'a very clean back room, in a very respectable house – where I am expected not to be at home in the day-time, unless poorly'. Houses like those on the Clapham Road were generally separated from the main road by substantial front gardens which may well have kept noise and dust at bay. Most of these gardens have disappeared, as the more prosperous tenants moved out at the end of the nineteenth century and shopkeepers moved in. These greengrocers, butchers, hardware storekeepers and general tradesmen built their business premises outwards over the vacant open space and lived over the new shop in what remained of the Georgian house.

The outlying old villages through which the roads leading out of London passed were also ripe for colonization by well-off Londoners in search of fresh air and well-drained soil. The northern heights seem to have proved especially popular with independent gentlemen and retired merchants alike. The 'little town of Barnet', an important staging post on the main road to Scotland and the north of England, is some 11 miles from Charing Cross and was therefore well beyond commuting distance in Dickens's time. It is now a Northern Line terminus, the centre of a large borough and, as a kind of northern border town, between London and the rest of the kingdom, High Barnet remains on the very fringe of the Green Belt. As Dickens noted in *Oliver Twist* in the 1830s 'every other house in Barnet was a tavern, large or small' but neither that, nor the presence of its famous, and unruly, livestock fair each early September, seem to have rendered it any less attractive as the kind of place a rich merchant or a professional gentleman might consider retiring to. There was a good deal of working farmland and meadowland just outside the town and in its immediate vicinity there were a number of substantial private mansions set in acres of landscaped park. Totally bereft of their rural context, some of these gentlemen's houses and villas, together with their truncated parks, survive as educational institutions in the new, extensive Borough of Barnet.

Even Finchley, 4 miles closer to the city, was still able to state its claim to semi-rustic seclusion until the 1860s. In *The Old Curiosity Shop* the bountiful Mr and Mrs Garland have a large 'cottage' at Finchley. Given its proximity to London, the Garlands' Abel Cottage seems to represent the kind of bucolic fantasy that was once known as *rus in urbe* ('the country in the town').

> It was a beautiful little cottage with a thatched roof and little spires at the gable-ends, and pieces of stained-glass in some of the windows, almost as large as pocket-books. On one side of the house was a little stable, just the size for the pony, with a little room over it ... White curtains were fluttering, and birds in cages that looked as bright as if they were made of gold, were singing, at the windows; plants were arranged on either side of the path, and clustered about the door; and the garden was bright with flowers in full bloom, which shed a sweet odour all round, and had a charming and elegant appearance.

Nothing, therefore, could be further from the smoky uniformity of middle-class London or the straggling untidiness of R. Wilfer's Holloway. This 'cottage' is also something of a step down from the gentlemen's mansions nearer to Barnet. Dickens himself approved sufficiently of the idyllic, countryfied nature of Finchley to have rented rooms at Cobley's Farm there in 1843. It was in this retreat, when he was working hard on *Martin Chuzzlewit*, that he conceived one of his most memorable London characters. John Forster, who joined Dickens at the cottage, tells us that it was 'here, walking and talking in the green lanes as the midsummer months were coming

Charles Dickens Museum

Cobley's Farm, Queen's Avenue, Finchley, *c.* 1900. Dickens rented rooms here in 1843 while he was working on *Martin Chuzzlewit.* The site is now marked by a plaque commemorating Dickens's stay here and the presumption that he invented the character of Mrs Gamp here

on, his introduction of Mrs Gamp ... first occurred to him'. The site of Cobley's Farm in Queen's Avenue, just to the north of the North Circular in Finchley, is marked with a plaque remembering both Dickens and Mrs Gamp.

Quite the grandest of the north London suburban mansions to survive into the twenty-first century is Kenwood House, south of Finchley on the road that links the villages of Hampstead and Highgate. In *Barnaby Rudge* it was 'Caen Wood', the seat of the Lord Chief Justice, Lord Mansfield, and hence the object of the destructive wrath of the more intrepid of the Gordon Rioters. They had already burned his house in Bloomsbury Square.

They marched away to ... Caen Wood, between Hampstead and Highgate, bent upon destroying that house likewise, and lighting up a great fire there, from which that height should be seen all over London. But in this they were disappointed, for, a party of horse having arrived before them, they retreated faster than they went, and came straight back to town.

Dickens knew both Hampstead and Highgate well. In 1832 he had lodged with a laundress, Mrs Davis, at North End, Hampstead, and with a Mrs Goodman 'next door to the Red Lion' in North Road, Highgate. In the early summer of 1837, while recuperating from the emotional trauma occasioned by the death of his young sister-in-law, Mary Hogarth, Dickens and his wife retreated to Collins's Farm (sometimes called Wylde's Farm) by the side of Hampstead Heath at North End. This part of north London was to figure dramatically in *Oliver Twist* when the frantic Bill Sikes fled from London after his murder of Nancy.

> He went through Islington; strode up the hill to Highgate on which there stands the stone in honour of Whittington; turned down Highgate Hill, unsteady of purpose, and uncertain where to go; struck off to the right again, almost as soon as he began to descend it; and taking the footpath across the fields, skirted Caen Wood and so came out on Hampstead Heath. Traversing the hollow by the Vale of Health, he mounted the opposite bank, and crossing the road which joins the villages of Hampstead and Highgate, made along the remaining portion of the heath to the fields at North End, in one of which he laid himself down under a hedge, and slept.

Thanks to the fact that Hampstead Heath and the leafy grounds of Kenwood are a public open space, much of Sikes's route can still be retraced. The breezy openness of the heath can still be relished much as Dickens himself relished it. As Forster recounts, he was particularly fond of a 'good brisk walk' from London uphill to Jack Straw's Castle, a tavern on the fringe of the heath 'where we can have a red-hot chop for dinner, and glass of good wine'.

David Copperfield shared Dickens's relish for healthy exercise. He would take a cold plunge in the old Roman bath in Strand Lane, off the Strand, before taking a walk to Hampstead in order to 'freshen' his wits. After breakfast (presumably at Jack Straw's) he would, like Dickens, walk back to London. David regularly visits the Steerforths' 'genteel old-fashioned house' in Highgate village. On his first visit he is struck by its being 'very quiet and orderly' and remarks on the fact that from his bedroom windows he can see 'all London lying in the distance like a great vapour, with here and there some lights twinkling through it'. The house Dickens was thinking of is commonly identified as Church House in South Grove. After his retirement from Canterbury, David's old head-master, Dr Strong, also ends up in a 'pretty old place' in Highgate, a cottage situated 'on the opposite side of the little town' from Mrs Steerforth's. So manifest were the attractions of this 'little town' that David resolves to rent his own small house as a marital home for his beloved Dora and her dog, Jip: 'I went into a cottage that I saw was to let, and examined it narrowly – for I felt it necessary to be practical. It would do for me and Dora admirably: with a little front garden for Jip to run about in, and bark at the tradespeople through the railings, and a capital room up-stairs for my aunt.'

On one of his walks up the now 'familiar' Highgate road he deter-mines that 'Dora was the reward, and Dora must be won.' Having won her, David and his new wife finally remove themselves to a 'pleasant' cottage close to the one he looked at earlier. It is a house that requires to be furnished (though all Dora ever buys for it is the Chinese pagoda, decorated with jingling bells, for Jip). Nevertheless, this is the marital home for which David has craved and his blissful recall of its interiors suggests that its furnishings are exactly what early Victorian newly-weds would have selected.

> Such a beautiful little house it is, with everything so bright and new; with the flowers on the carpets looking as if freshly gath-ered, and the green leaves on the paper as if they had just come out; with the spotless muslin curtains, and the blushing rose-coloured furniture … and everybody tumbling over Jip's Pagoda, which is much too big for the establishment.

Apart from the nuisance of Jip's pagoda, this is an epitome of unpretentious, bourgeois, suburban comfort, replete with polished rosewood tables and flowery Axminster carpets. In *David Copperfield*, Highgate Village, serene on its hilltop, is portrayed as quintessentially suburban – close enough to London for the convenience of the brisk walker, yet pleasantly above the city's smoke and detached from the sprawl of Holloway and Camden Town.

Southwards and Westwards along the Thames

When David is first smitten with Dora she is living with her lawyer father, Mr Spenlow, in his villa at Norwood, in what was then the county of Surrey. Apart from the fact that it has a conservatory filled with geraniums, we know little of the architecture of this villa, but it very probably resembled the house owned by Mr Carker in the same area. Dickens carefully describes Carker's neat villa in Chapter 33 of *Dombey and Son*. It is 'situated in the green and wooded country near Norwood' and it seems to be far newer and far sprucer than anything Highgate Village might have offered. It also has a far more expansive garden around it.

> It is not a mansion; it is of no pretensions as to size; but it is beautifully arranged, and tastefully kept. The lawn, the soft smooth slope, the flower-garden, the clumps of trees where graceful forms of ash and willow are not wanting, the conservatory, the rustic verandah with sweet-smelling creeping plants entwined about the pillars, the simple exterior of the house, the well-ordered offices, though all upon the diminutive scale proper to a mere cottage, bespeak an amount of elegant comfort within, that might serve for a palace ... Rich colours, excellently blended, meet the eye at every turn; in the furniture – its proportions admirably devised to suit the shapes and sizes of the small rooms; on the walls; upon the floors; tinging and subduing the light that comes through the odd glass doors and windows here and there. There are a few choice prints and pictures, too; in quaint nooks and recesses there is no want of books; and there are games of skill and chance set forth on tables...

This, therefore, is the house of a well-off man of taste, one with pretensions to high culture. Yet, as Dickens is at pains to suggest, the carpets are too soft, the taste is often verging on the 'voluptuous' and the books are more impressive for their bindings than for their content. It is also all a bit too tidy, too sensuous and too contrived to suggest either real comfort or an owner who is truly at ease with his surroundings. Carker, with his toothsome smile, is after all one of the most unpleasant and corrupt characters in *Dombey and Son*. His villa, its outbuildings and its interiors are, as far as we can tell, representative of how the bourgeois residents of Norwood once lived.

That leafy, outer-suburban world of the Spenlows, the Carkers and their like is lost for ever. Apart from its hilly topography, there is very little surviving in modern Norwood that might recall the bosky idyll that Dickens describes in his novels of the late 1840s. The Crystal Palace was rebuilt on Sydenham Hill in 1854, and for the rest of the nineteenth century massive crowds were drawn to its attractions. The frequent trains that served the extended Norwood area also both destroyed its old seclusion and steadily changed its social and architectural complexion.

When Mr Spenlow dies, his daughter, Dora, is obliged to move in with her prim maiden aunts in Putney. In the 1840s Putney was regarded as a respectable if somewhat nondescript suburb, of little architectural or topographical distinction apart from its pleasant position on the south bank of the River Thames. It was directly opposite Fulham on the north bank, to which it was linked by an eighteenth-century wooden toll bridge. It was, however, a popular enough spot with Thames rowers. David Copperfield, romantically obsessed with Dora, manages to 'haunt' the place, but later wonders how he ever found the time to do so. In Chapter 41 he tells us that he and Traddles walked there from London in order to pay their respects to Dora's two maiden aunts. It would seem likely that David and Dora were married in Putney Parish Church. Dickens is unspecific as to location, but the church concerned certainly seems to have had a distinctly riverside ambience; David seems to remember it only through the haze of a bridegroom's nervous anticipation:

The church is calm enough … The rest is all more or less incoherent dream … of the clergyman and clerk appearing; of a few boatmen and some other people strolling in; of an ancient mariner behind me, strongly flavouring the church with rum … of my walking so proudly and lovingly down the aisle with my sweet wife upon my arm, through a mist of half-seen people, pulpits, monuments, pews, fonts, organs, and church-windows…

The body of Putney Church was rebuilt in 1836 and yet again in the 1870s so we are unlikely to recognize any of the church furniture represented in the illustration of David's wedding that Phiz provided for the first edition of the novel. His etching does, however, capture the feel of an 'incoherent' Gothic dream of an extraordinarily cluttered church, though it omits both the stray boatmen and the rum-sodden mariner.

On the opposite side of the Thames to Putney is Fulham, a village which in Dickens's time was famed for the beauty of its river-side walk on the flank of the Bishop of London's park, and for the villas and their lush gardens which lay beyond the park. The most celebrated of these, Craven Cottage, was the home of Dickens's friend, Edward Bulwer-Lytton. The Fulham Palace and its park survive, but the villas are long gone (though the name of Craven Cottage lingers as that of Fulham Football Club's ground). One of the riverside villas is supposed to have been the residence of Sir Barnet and Lady Skettles in *Dombey and Son*.

Sir Barnet and Lady Skettles, very good people, resided in a pretty villa at Fulham, on the banks of the Thames; which was one of the most desirable residences in the world when a rowing-match happened to be going past, but had its little inconveniences at other times, among which may be enumerated the occasional appearance of the river in the drawing-room, and the contemporaneous disappearance of the lawn and shrubbery.

It is while Florence Dombey is staying with the Skettles that she walks 'up and down the river's bank' in the early mornings medi-tating on her loneliness and her rejection by her father. She regularly notices 'a very poor man' who also roams the riverbanks accompanied by a sullen and indifferent girl child. This father never lets his daughter out of his sight, though the child gives no responsive sign of any return of his profound attachment. It is a reverse of her own painful situation. Strange, melancholy and contrived this incident may be, but it comes to have a key role in Florence's own emotional education.

There are other desirable riverside residences in Dickens's novels. In *Great Expectations* Herbert Pocket's parents have a house at Hammersmith with a garden overlooking the river. Here Pip lodges in order to improve his manners and to smooth away his rustic edges. At Hammersmith he meets Bentley Drummle, and, in imitation of Drummle and his friend Startop, Pip and Herbert buy a half-share in a rowing boat that they take out on the Thames in the evenings. Pip, however, confesses that he was obliged to relearn his boating skills in accordance with his new gentlemanly pretensions:

> I was pretty good at most exercises in which country-boys are adepts, but, as I was conscious of wanting elegance of style for the Thames – not to say for other waters – I at once engaged to place myself under the tuition of the winner of a prize-wherry who plied our stairs ... This practical authority confused me very much, by saying I had the arm of a blacksmith. If he could have known how nearly the compliment lost him his pupil, I doubt if he would have paid it.

The Pockets were clearly good tutors in giving this former black-smith's apprentice so acute a consciousness of the defectiveness of his country ways. Pip, who has retained the rooms he shares with Herbert at Barnard's Inn, goes 'backwards and forwards' to London in order to get accustomed to 'certain places in London' where he might acquire 'such mere rudiments as I wanted'. He walks, of course, and confesses to having grown fond of the route he would have taken through Kensington ('though it is not so pleasant a road as it was then'). This, incidentally, would have been the same, once open, road through Kensington and Hammersmith, and then on to Chiswick, Kew and Brentford, which Oliver is forced to take by Bill Sikes in Chapter 21 of *Oliver Twist*.

When, early in *Little Dorrit* Arthur Clennam is invited to visit Mr Meagles at his riverside villa at Twickenham, he walks via Fulham and Putney 'for the pleasure of strolling over the heath'. Dickens probably means Putney Heath. It is here that Arthur's regular walking pace sets him thinking in a classically Dickensian manner:

> It was bright and shining there; and when he found himself so far on his road to Twickenham, he found himself a long way on his road to a number of airier and less substantial destinations. They had risen before him fast, in the healthful exercise and the pleasant road. It is not easy to walk alone in the country, without musing upon something. And he had plenty of unsettled subjects to meditate upon, though he had been walking to Land's End.

Arthur must have had plenty of time to 'stroll' to Twickenham in those pre-railway years. It was certainly not Land's End but it *was* some 10 miles from Hyde Park Corner by road.

When he arrives at Mr Meagles's 'cottage-residence' he finds it:

> ... a charming place (none the worse for being a little eccentric), on the road by the river, and just what the residence of the Meagles family ought to be. It stood in a garden ... and it was defended by a goodly show of handsome trees and spreading evergreens ... It was made out of an old brick house, of which part had been pulled down, and another part had been changed into the present cottage; so there was a hale elderly portion ... and a young, picturesque, very pretty portion ... There was even the later addition of a conservatory sheltering itself against it, uncertain of hue in its deep stained glass, and in its more transparent portions flashing to the sun's rays ... Within view was the peaceful river and the ferry-boat.

Dickens associates this 'cottage-residence's' eccentricities and structural oddities with the nature of the Meagles family. Despite its manifest charms, like the Meagles family it is somehow a little too much of a good thing.

Whether or not such a structure was representative of early nine-

179

teenth-century Twickenham it is now difficult to tell. A guidebook to the environs of London published soon after Dickens's death noted that the village and its surrounds had always been 'a favourite residence' and that it boasted a greater number of 'noted houses and eminent inhabitants' than almost any other village on the Thames. With 'the advent of the railway and the progress of the builder', this guidebook added, much of the rural seclusion and gentlemanly exclusiveness that Dickens would have known had steadily been diminished. Viewed from the River Thames, however, this part of London still retains some real charm.

Eastwards to Docklands and Greenwich

As Pip's reacquisition, and necessary refinement, of his rowing skills suggests to us, there were two distinct ways of regarding the River Thames in Dickens's day. There was the working river and there was the river dedicated to pleasure. There was a part of the river where men and women toiled by and on the water, and there was a part where gentlemen took their lady friends boating. In *Great Expectations* Pip may have to learn a different way of sculling in order not to embarrass his gentlemen friends, but in *Our Mutual Friend* the working-class Lizzie Hexam's old ability to manoeuvre a working rowing boat proves to be a life-saver. Although she has moved westwards into rustic Berkshire, a long way upstream from her riverside origins at Limehouse, she readily takes to the water:

> A sure touch of her old practised hand, a sure step of her old prac-tised foot, a sure light balance of the body, and she was in the boat. A quick glance of her practised eye showed her, even through the deep dark shadow, the sculls in a rack … Another moment, and she had cast off (taking the line with her), and the boat had shot out into the moonlight, and she was rowing down the stream as never other woman rowed on English water.

For Lizzie, the rescue of the battered and drowning Eugene Wrayburn from the Thames is proof of a love that is stronger than death. It is also proof, if ever we needed it, that Lizzie is true to her roots and her experience.

Reading Dickens's novels, it would be wrong to assume that there was an easy distinction between the working Thames and the pleasurable Thames. The Thames was a working river from its mouth until it became a mere stripling in Oxfordshire. Coal barges and other small trading vessels were ubiquitous. What was generally true, however, was that there were great houses, villas, boathouses and jetties where the Thames was 'pleasant' upstream, and there were great docks, mud-clogged quays, warehouses and run-down properties downstream where it was 'industrial'. Though he barely describes them, London's docks were one of the wonders of the world when Dickens was alive. Foreign visitors were often staggered not only by the amount of shipping on the river but also by the great dock buildings. Take, for example, the almost breathless description given by Friedrich Engels in his *The Condition of the Working Class in England*:

I know nothing more imposing than the view which the Thames offers during the ascent from the sea to London Bridge. The masses of building, the wharves on both sides ... the countless ships along both shores, crowding ever closer together, until, at last, only a narrow passage remains in the middle of the river, a passage through which hundreds of steamers shoot by one another; all this is so vast, so impressive, that a man cannot collect himself, but is lost in the marvel of England's greatness before he sets foot on English soil.

The great docks to which Engels refers were the product of the commercial enterprise and the engineering sophistication of the first half of the nineteenth century. The London and the East India Docks on the north side of the river opened in 1805 and the Surrey Docks on the south side in 1807. They were followed by the St Katharine's Docks, east of the Tower, in 1828, the West India South in 1829–33 and the Royal Victoria in 1855. Each enclosed vast basins of water, each boasted blocks of warehouses constructed on an unprecedented scale, and, on the landward side, each was surrounded by stark brick walls intended to deter unwanted intruders. The Royal Victoria Dock, begun in 1850 and financed by railway entrepreneurs, had 94 acres of water and was the largest of its kind in the world.

Even though Dickens tended to set his novels in the London of the 1820s and 1830s he made scant use of this vast area of new commercial enterprise. Even when his would-be emigrant characters set sail, they tend to leave from Gravesend, the entrance to the Port of London and 30 miles downstream. Until 1825 it was at Gravesend that all outward-bound vessels from London received their final clearances. Mr Micawber and his family, bound for Australia, leave London initially from Hungerford Stairs at Charing Cross (the very mention of which must have sent a shiver down Dickens's spine). They board their ship at Gravesend (where David Copperfield visits them and the Peggotty party on deck). When Pip attempts to smuggle Magwitch out of London it is again by hailing a Continental steamer at Gravesend. He does, however, give us a fine description in *Great Expectations* of the dense commercial traffic on the early-nineteenth-century Thames:

> At that time, the steam-traffic on the Thames was far below its present extent, and the watermen's boats were far more numerous. Of barges, sailing colliers, and coasting-traders, there were perhaps as many as now; but, of steam-ships, great and small, not a tithe or a twentieth part so many ... Old London Bridge was soon passed, and old Billingsgate market with its oyster-boats and Dutchmen, and the White Tower and Traitor's Gate, and we were in among the tiers of shipping ... here were colliers by the score and score ... here, at her moorings was to-morrow's steamer for Rotterdam, of which we took good notice; and here to-morrow's for Hamburg, under whose bowsprit we crossed.

As Pip insists, 'The navigation between bridges, in an open boat, was a much easier and commoner matter in those days than it is in these'. His reference to the old London Bridge, which was replaced in 1824–31, helps us to date his description. There were also far fewer of the paddle-steamers which would have been familiar to

Our Mutual Friend links east London with west London, East End characters with West End characters. In it territorial boundaries are regularly dissolved and class barriers are purposefully crossed. The newly built schools where Bradley Headstone teaches are situated 'down in that district of the flat country tending to the Thames, where Kent and Surrey meet' and even here the railways on their viaducts will gradually kill off the old market gardens. London is in a state of flux between the old and the new, between the known and the still unknown. *Our Mutual Friend* is a novel set almost exclusively in a London where the murky loops of the tidal Thames make for juxtapositions between the south bank and the north, and where the regular flow from west to east is reversed by strong tides. The novel's characters freely move both upstream and downstream, northwards and southwards. They cross the river by bridges, pleasure boats and rowing boats. They make a living from its waters, and sometimes they drown in them.

The novel opens 'in these times of ours', midstream on the river, and with a dirty rowing boat floating between Southwark Bridge and London Bridge. Lizzie Hexam is rowing as her father intently watches the rising tide. In the bottom of their dirty boat there is a 'rotten stain ... which bore some resemblance to the outline of a muffled human form, coloured as though with diluted blood'. Gaffer Hexam, 'the nightbird of the Thames', is a scavenger, and he has found the carrion he most relishes: a man's dead body. It is small wonder that the twentieth-century poet T. S. Eliot considered using a seemingly inconsequential quotation from *Our Mutual Friend* as the title for the first part of his poem, 'The Waste Land'. Both the poem and the novel open either by or on London Bridge, and both ponder the disturbance to the living presented by the dead, or more specifically, a drowned man.

Gaffer Hexam lives by the river beyond Ratcliffe and Rotherhithe on a stretch of the Limehouse river bank 'where the accumulated scum of humanity seemed to be washed from higher ground'. His conical timber house has the look of having once been a windmill, there being 'a rotten wart of wood upon its forehead that seemed to indicate where the sails had been'. His fellow scavenger and arch-rival, Rogue Riderhood, lives nearby in 'deep and

Charles Dickens Museum

Limehouse Reach, c. 1900. This haunting photograph suggests both the bleakness and the workaday quality of the lower reaches of the Thames. This is the world of Gaffer Hexam in *Our Mutual Friend*

dark Limehouse Hole, among the riggers, and the mast, oar, and block-makers, and the boat-builders and the sail-lofts'. This is no longer the breezy and busy Limehouse where Dickens located Captain Cuttle's lodgings in *Dombey and Son*. The area now seems infinitely more decayed and infinitely more sinister.

Very few of the rickety wooden buildings that might have suggested Hexam's defunct mill or Riderhood's hovel to Dickens have survived the nineteenth century. What has survived is a venerable public house in Narrow Street in Limehouse called the Grapes. This may well be the original of Dickens's eccentrically named tavern, the Six Jolly Fellowship Porters:

> The Six Jolly Fellowship Porters … a tavern of a dropsical appearance, had long settled down into a state of hale infirmity. In its whole constitution it had not a straight floor, and hardly a straight line; but it had outlasted and clearly would outlast, many a better-trimmed building, many a sprucer public-house. Externally, it was a narrow lop-sided wooden jumble of corpulent windows, heaped one upon another as you might heap as many

'The Grapes', Limehouse, c. 1900. Readily recognizable today from the River Thames, this is probably the original of the 'Six Jolly Fellowship Porters' in *Our Mutual Friend*. Its hinterland is now far less seedy, though far more bland, than in Dickens's day

Charles Dickens Museum

toppling oranges, with a crazy wooden verandah impending over the water ... The back of this establishment, though the chief entrance was there, so contracted, that it merely represented in its connexion with the front, the handle of a flat-iron set upright on its broadest end. This handle stood at the bottom of a wilderness of court and alley ...

The 'wilderness of court and alley' has largely disappeared from the hinterland of the now gentrified Narrow Street, but its surviving old houses and converted warehouses still suggest something of a proper 'Dickensian' ambience. The Grapes, which is seen to best advantage from the River Thames, even boasts a Dickens Bar.

Passing river boats, plying their way to and from Greenwich, tend to point out the Grapes to twenty-first-century tourists. As readers familiar with *Our Mutual Friend* will recognize, similar river journeys on paddle-steamers to Greenwich were very familiar to most Victorian Londoners. Small steamboats had become the normal way of moving up and down the Thames by the third decade of the nineteenth century, regularly covering the 18 miles between Richmond in the west and Woolwich in the east. Downstream, they permitted travellers to observe not just the decaying wooden relics of the old riverside, but also the serried masts of the ocean-going shipping and the great, spare buildings and warehouses of the new docks. Fares varied from between 1d and 6d (depending on the distance travelled) and passengers from central London were able to pick up the boats at landing stages at London, Southwark, Blackfriars, Waterloo, Hungerford and Westminster Bridges.

Greenwich proved a singularly popular destination for parties of ladies and gentlemen, owing to the singular culinary attractions of its riverside taverns. These establishments were celebrated for their whitebait dinners, the fish being supposedly freshly caught in the river. The most celebrated of these taverns were the Ship, west of the Greenwich Hospital, and the Trafalgar, the Yacht and the Crown and Sceptre to its east. Alas, only the Trafalgar survives. It was built in 1837 and, after some sixty years of neglect, has been restored to its old function. The Ship, which was regularly patronized by Dickens and his friends, fell victim to bombing during the Second World War. It was at Greenwich that Dickens was fêted in 1842 when he arrived back in London after his long trip to America. In May 1843 the novelist himself did the honours by hosting a dinner for John Black, the editor of the liberal newspaper, *The Morning Chronicle*, and, later in the same summer, the completion of *Martin Chuzzlewit* was celebrated here by what one guest termed a 'christening dinner'. It was on this occasion that the painter Turner was present, and John Forster records that the great man refused to remove 'a huge red, belcher-handerkerchief' in which he had swathed his neck despite the heat of a sultry day.

It is to Greenwich that John Harmon, Bella Wilfer, and her father Reginald Wilfer privily resort in Chapter 4 of the last book of *Our Mutual Friend*. Having left on 'an early steamboat' from one

Charles Dickens Museum

Trafalgar Tavern, Greenwich, *c.* 1900. A great favourite of Dickens's contemporaries, famous for its whitebait suppers

of the London piers, John is married to Bella at Greenwich Parish Church. They have declined to tell Bella's disapproving mother of the arrangements, and only do so once the wedding is well and truly over. After the wedding at St Alphege's, they have breakfast and then take a ride and a stroll on Blackheath 'among heath and bloom'. To crown the day they have dinner at the Ship, in the same little room where, earlier in the novel, Bella and her father had eaten, 'overlooking the river … looking at the ships and steamboats'. In one of his most delightful fantasies, Dickens makes it clear that this particular wedding supper is not limited to freshly caught whitebait.

> What a dinner! Specimens of all the fishes that swim in the sea, surely had swum their way to it, and if samples of the fishes of divers colours that made a speech in the Arabian Nights … and then jumped out of the frying-pan, were not to be recognized, it was only because they had all become of one hue by being cooked in batter among the whitebait. And the dishes being seasoned

with Bliss – an article which they are sometimes out of, at Greenwich – were of perfect flavour, and the golden drinks had been bottled in the golden age and hoarding up their sparkles ever since.

When Dickens refers to one of the stories from the *Arabian Nights*, which he frequently does in his fiction, we know that he is alerting his readers to a particular magic. Here the magic is purely and serenely benign. The dust, the decay, the murk and the mud that have tainted so much of the atmosphere of the London of *Our Mutual Friend* have here been dissipated by love and good company.

John Harmon and his new wife have selected a 'bright and fresh' cottage at Blackheath, on the steep hill above Greenwich, as their marital home. Blackheath was well known to Dickens for across the heath itself passed the old Dover Road. This was the main road to and from Kent and, some 25 miles away, lay Dickens's house at Gad's Hill Place, near Rochester. Dickens was familiar with it both as a passenger and as a pedestrian. On one sleepless night in October 1857 he had left his bed at Tavistock House at two in the morning and had walked to Gad's Hill along this lonely road (it took him seven hours). In his Christmas story of 1854, 'The Seven Poor Travellers', he describes a winter's walk in the other direction (though the story ends with the narrator descending through 'the long vista of gnarled old trees in Greenwich Park' in order to catch the train into London for the last short leg of the journey). Just beyond Blackheath was the step incline of Shooter's Hill, up which the Dover Mail lumbers at the opening of *A Tale of Two Cities*, and somewhere near here was Salem House, the rum school conducted by Mr Creakle to which David Copperfield is sent by his stepfather.

To Victorian Londoners, the heights of Blackheath and the adjacent Greenwich Park were famed for the fine views they afforded over London. These views were readily accessible to the newly married Harmons from their Blackheath cottage. Like David and Dora Copperfield at Highgate, they would be able to look down on the panorama of smoky, working London spread out before them. They are of the metropolis, but also detached from it. In the first decade of the nineteenth century the superb prospect of London from Greenwich had been painted by J. M. W. Turner, an artist whose work was greatly admired by Dickens. Turner's painting shows deer in the foreground and then, at the bottom of the hill, Wren's domed Greenwich Hospital. Beyond it the Thames winds away, past the undeveloped scrubland of the Isle of Dogs, through the developing docks to the hazy expanse of the great city in the distance. We move, therefore, from a deer park on the very edge of built-up London to the heart of the metropolis itself. When his painting had been first exhibited in 1809 Turner had attached verses to it deploring what he regarded as the ugly sprawl of modern London, but these verses could not render the prospect he had painted any less impressive. What makes Turner's picture instantly recognizable as a representation of London, however, is not the loops of its river or the straggling detritus of its industry or its encroaching urban sprawl, but the unmistakeable profile of the dome of St Paul's. The cathedral rises greyly in the distance above the haze, clustered around by the myriad spires of the City's churches. Turner's view of London from Greenwich suggests magnificence as well as squalor, space as well as smoke, the peace of the park as much as the distant, restless energy of the city. Like the city that Dickens describes, this is a London that has been transfigured by art.

Mostly *Little Dorrit*

THIS RELATIVELY SHORT walk (about 2 miles all told) runs northwards from Elephant and Castle underground station (Northern and Bakerloo Lines) to Bank station in the City (Northern, Central and District and Circle Lines, with links to the Docklands Light Railway – DLR).

Emerging from Elephant and Castle tube station follow signs for Newington Causeway. The Elephant area was physically transformed in the 1960s and is about to be transformed again. It is not easy to find one's way around this 'ganglion of roads' as Dickens so aptly describes it in *Bleak House*. It is now an untidy roundabout into which five major roads feed. We are going to head north to the City, but westward lies the road to Westminster and to the north west is Blackfriars Road where stood the *Surrey Theatre*, where in *Little Dorrit* Frederick Dorrit played 'a clarionet as dirty as himself' and where Fanny Dorrit performed as a dancer. To the south-east lies the *New Kent Road*, along which David Copperfield walks on his way to Dover. Having been robbed of his box and his half-guinea he pauses on a doorstep to recollect himself. Webb's County Terrace, where David pauses, has long been demolished but the 'great foolish image' of a cherub blowing a shell, which once stood in front of the terrace, survived until recently in damaged form in a scrubby garden on the site.

In the middle of the Elephant and Castle roundabout, and somewhat perilous to reach, there is an outsized metal box which is intended to commemorate Dickens's great contemporary, the pioneering scientist Michael Faraday, who was born hereabouts in 1794.

County Terrace, New Kent Road, *c.* 1900. Formerly Webb's County Terrace. David Copperfield pauses to rest here by the 'great foolish image' of a cherub blowing a shell. The terrace is long gone and the cherub has been removed

Charles Dickens Museum

Newington Causeway is now a somewhat nondescript thorough-fare which passes under a heavy railway bridge. Hardly any buildings of Dickens's time survive. After a few minutes' walk, however, we find to the right the *Inner London Crown Court* which replaced the old Surrey Sessions House constructed in 1791. The present stone building, set back from the road, dates only from 1921, though the concrete extensions of 1977 do little to enhance it. Behind the original Court House stood the Surrey County Gaol of 1791–9, commonly known as the *Horsemonger Lane Gaol*. Horsemonger Lane was a narrow turning to the right which led into what is now Harper Road. The site of the gaol, which closed in 1878 and was demolished two years later, is now a small park shaded by mature trees. There is a notice about the site's history in the park. Dickens knew the old gaol well and witnessed the public execution of Mr and Mrs Manning here in 1849. The Mannings, found guilty of murdering their lodger, were hanged on a gibbet erected on the top of the old gatehouse. Dickens's horrified account of the execution and of the behaviour of the spectators at the event is quoted in Chapter 3.

None of the old houses whose front windows were rented out to the ghouls who came to see the Mannings die now survives. But there is a pleasant range of Georgian houses in Bath Terrace, which in turn leads into the intact *Trinity Church Square*, which dates from 1824–32. The deconsecrated Greek Revival church in the middle of the square was built in 1823–4 and now serves as an orchestral rehearsal room. The much eroded fourteenth-century stone statue of a king which stands in front of the church is reputedly of King Alfred. It was moved here from Westminster Hall in 1822.

Returning to Newington Causeway at its junction with Harper Road we can cross to the site of the *King's Bench Prison* where Mr Micawber was incarcerated for debt in *David Copperfield*. *Stone's End Street* marks its eastern boundary. The so-called 'liberties' of the prison stretched for some 3 miles beyond the walls and the debtor-father of Madeline Bray in *Nicholas Nickleby* actually lived in a house near *St George's Circus*. In the 1840s the debtors' prison (by now renamed Queen's Bench) was closed and amalgamated with the Fleet and Marshalsea Gaols, but the building continued in use as a military prison. It was demolished in 1880.

At this crossroads Newington Causeway changes its name to *Borough High Street*. We continue walking northwards. On the left is *Lant Street*, which is described in *Pickwick Papers* as a place where 'the majority of the inhabitants either direct their energies to the letting of furnished apartments or devote themselves to the healthful and invigorating pursuit of mangling'. Here, at No. 1 (later changed to No. 5), Dickens lodged as a boy in 1824 when his father was in the nearby Marshalsea Prison. Dickens's lodgings, now demolished, consisted of a back attic overlooking a timber yard. Although Dickens later claimed that this brief period of independence represented a 'paradise', he was to allot the same accommodation to Bob Sawyer in *Pickwick Papers* and to David Copperfield. The site is now occupied by a block of modern apartments. There is a Charles Dickens School further along Lant Street, and some of the streets beyond it have now been given a series of

Dickensian names (Weller, Copperfield, Doyce, Dorrit, Clennam, Sawyer), though none has an immediate connection with the novelist.

Returning to Borough High Street and continuing northwards we reach Borough underground station, where we cross *Marshalsea Road* and Borough High Street to the prominently sited church of *St George the Martyr*. The present church, with its stone spire, dates from 1734–6 and was built to the design of the otherwise obscure architect John Price. It replaced a medieval parish church. It is not often open, but its interior is worth exploring (though there is little surviving from its original furnishings). The modern stained glass in the east window contains a small representation of Amy Dorrit. In Dickens's novel Amy is christened in this church and she and Maggy are obliged to spend the night in the vestry here when they are locked out of the Marshalsea. Amy and Arthur Clennam are married here in the last chapter of *Little Dorrit*, and from the steps

Charles Dickens Museum

Borough High Street, c. 1900. These buildings would have been familiar to Dickens as a boy and as an adult. They are typical of nineteenth-century London's admixture of structures dating from the seventeenth century onwards

197

at the west end of the church she and Arthur descend 'to a modest life of usefulness and happiness … into the roaring streets, inseparable and blest'.

Behind St George's is the former parish burying ground, which has now been transformed into a small park. The brick wall to the north of this park is the old wall of the *Marshalsea Prison*. The medieval prison moved to this site in 1811 to hold debtors and petty offenders (though two cells were reserved for smugglers). Dickens's father was incarcerated here as a debtor in February 1824 and was released on 28 May of the same year. This short but shameful period in the history of the Dickens family left deep scars, especially on the future novelist. The period of John Dickens's imprisonment and of young Charles's employment at Warren's Blacking at Charing Cross seems to have been covered up and was certainly not mentioned in public. Dickens appears to have told only his friend John Forster about the Marshalsea period. No biographical notice of Dickens written during his lifetime contains a hint of the disgrace. The facts only became public

Charles Dickens Museum

Borough High Street, c. 1890. These buildings, on the site of the Marshalsea Prison, are now long gone

after the publication of the first volume of Forster's *Life of Charles Dickens* in 1872. Forster was thus able to give both *David Copperfield* and *Little Dorrit* a significant biographical context.

The best way to view the site of the Marshalsea Prison is to continue along Borough High Street and to turn left up the narrow *Angel Court*, which runs parallel to the old wall. We are now in what was an open area of the old prison. Its stiflingly cramped condition, where William Dorrit is incarcerated for debt, and where his son and two daughters lodge with him, is vividly and depressingly described in *Little Dorrit* in 1857: 'It was an oblong pile of barrack building, partitioned into squalid houses standing back to back, so that there were no back rooms; environed by a narrow paved yard, hemmed in by high walls duly spiked on top.' The gaol was long gone when Dickens wrote this account, but the barrack blocks survived. Nowadays, despite the absence of the barracks and the spikes on the wall, much of the melancholy atmosphere survives. Dickens again described the old Marshalsea in the preface to the novel. The account is more than a little disingenuous. No mention is made of his own family's association with the place, but much of his emotion is transferred to the fictional Dorrits.

> Whosoever goes into Marshalsea Place, turning out of Angel Court leading to Bermondsey, will find his feet on the very paving stones of the extinct Marshalsea Gaol; will see its narrow yard to the right and to the left, very little altered, if at all, except that the walls were lowered when the place got free; will look upon the rooms in which the debtors lived; will stand among the crowding ghosts of many miserable years.

We now know that for Charles Dickens these 'crowding ghosts' were more than imagined.

The name of Angel Court reminds us of the succession of old inns that once lined both sides of Borough High Street. The most famous, Geoffrey Chaucer's Tabard Inn, where the pilgrims to Canterbury assembled before departing on their journey through Kent, finally disappeared only in 1873. It stood in *Talbot Yard*. The names of other yards on the east side of the road remind us of other

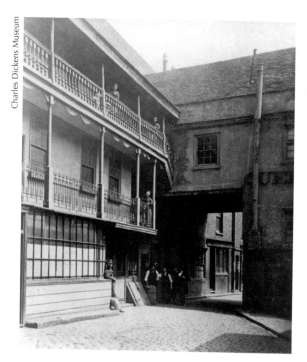

Charles Dickens Museum

The Queen's Head, Borough High Street *c.* 1880. This fine galleried inn and its yard were demolished in 1886

lost inns (the Queen's Head, the Three Tuns, the Mermaid, the White Hart, the King's Head). These alleys were once the entrances to inn yards, serving the carts and coaches travelling to Rochester, Canterbury and Dover. They now mostly back onto the ancillary buildings of Guy's Hospital, though occasionally some battered woodwork suggests the world of horse transport and of coaches and wagons pushing their way from a cramped space into the busy thoroughfare beyond. The one great survival is *The George*, or rather the impressive fragment of the galleried George Inn (77 Borough High Street).

In Dickens's day many of the old inns retained their original architecture and their key function as a hub of the national transport network. This function declined rapidly with the advent of the railways. Dickens describes these Inns in *Pickwick Papers* as 'great, rambling, queer, old places ... with galleries, and passages, and staircases'. There were bars, a coffee room, services and stabling on the ground floor but the bedrooms leading off the galleries above were somewhat reminiscent of modern American motels. Like motels they provided accommodation for customers who were on the move. Mr Pickwick memorably encounters Sam Weller at the White Hart, where Sam is employed in livery as a 'boots' (the cleaner of customers' footwear). *The George* (which is passingly referred to in *Little Dorrit*) provides the most substantial survival of these once familiar London inns. The present building dates from 1676 but it lost two of its three wings when they were demolished by a railway company in 1899. Its interiors are delightfully cramped and creaky, and serve to shut out the latter-day architectural intrusions which mar the inn-yard.

Continuing northwards along Borough High Street, we reach *St Thomas's Street*, which leads to the old quadrangle of *Guy's Hospital* (where Dickens's Bob Sawyer, of Lant Street, was 'a carver and cutter of live people's bodies'). Opposite the hospital entrance is a fine range of seventeenth-century houses and the now de-consecrated *St Thomas's Church* (rebuilt in 1702–3 and now serving as a

The George, Borough High Street. This nineteenth-century photograph shows the inn when its courtyard was used as a railway goods yard

chapter house for Southwark Cathedral). The church once formed part of the entrance court to St Thomas's Hospital. Its attic was used as the hospital's herb-garret, where medicinal herbs were dried and stored. This can be visited along with the part of the attic which was converted into an operating theatre in 1821. The restored operating theatre provides us with a salutary reminder of the state of medical science in Dickens's day. The church adjoins a handsome stone block of 1842, situated at an angle to Borough High Street, which is the only other surviving part of the old St Thomas's Hospital, which moved to a new site opposite the Houses of Parliament in 1868–71. Much of the old site had been acquired by the Charing Cross Railway Company and disappeared under the buildings of London Bridge Station, which was built in 1840–4, and rebuilt in 1849. From here Dickens regularly travelled to France; his first trip was on the South Eastern Railway's Double Special Express Service in 1850. It took him twelve hours to get to Paris by train and steamship, and his delight in the speed and efficiency of the service is described in his essay 'A Flight' of August 1851.

There is now little in the much reconstructed station area to detain a Dickensian walker, but if we cross Borough High Street and go down the steps to Southwark Cathedral we can still capture something of the feel of the London Dickens might have recognized. Much has changed thanks to the railway, but it was the rebuilding of London Bridge in 1823–31 that had the most radical effect. The boy Dickens would have known the old bridge, which had lost the houses which made it celebrated in 1758–62. This medieval bridge, having been deemed no longer fit for purpose, was replaced by a new granite structure designed by John Rennie, upstream from the old one, which was opened with great ceremony on 1 August 1831. The approach to the new bridge on the Southwark side required the removal of the easternmost chapels of the cathedral. This second bridge was in turn replaced in 1967–72 by the present concrete structure. The handsome old bridge was sold and reconstructed stone by stone in the Arizona desert at Lake Havasu City. It is a wonderful incongruity that so urban a structure should end up in such a relatively empty and dry place.

Dickens would have known Southwark Cathedral as St Saviour's Parish Church; it only became a cathedral in 1897. Having lost its medieval eastern chapels for a road-widening scheme in 1830, its ancient nave was unroofed and demolished in 1838. The replacement nave Dickens knew was a gimcrack affair. This sad relic of a great church only regained its proper dignity in the 1890s when the nave was rebuilt in anticipation of its new status. Inside, many writers associated with the Borough (as Southwark is known) are commemorated in monuments and in stained glass. Alas, there is no memorial to Dickens's very considerable (though often sad) associations with the area.

Behind the cathedral, off *Montague Close*, can be found the last remains of the granite arches and vaults which provided the approach to the new London Bridge. If we return to street level and begin to cross the bridge we can look down to the site of the steps where Nancy makes her disclosures about Oliver Twist to Rose Maylie and Mr Brownlow. She is overheard by Noah Claypole, hidden in an angle of the wall, and this leads directly to Nancy's brutal murder.

> The steps ... which were those which, on the Surrey bank, and on the same side of the bridge as St Saviour's Church, form a landing-stairs from the river ... These stairs are a part of the bridge; they consist of three flights. Just below the end of the second, going down, the stone wall on the left terminates in an ornamental pilaster facing towards the Thames. At this point the lower steps widen so that a person turning that angle of the wall is necessarily unseen by any others on the stairs who chance to be above him, if only a step.

The sensation of standing where Nancy and Noah Claypole did can now only be experienced under the blazing Arizona sun of Lake Havasu City!

London Bridge was often described by Dickens for it remained one of London's most significant crossing points between the still populous City of London and the southern suburbs. Famously *Our Mutual Friend* begins 'as an autumn evening is closing in' on the

Charles Dickens Museum

London Bridge steps, *c.* 1900. These are the steps made famous by Dickens in *Oliver Twist*, for it is here that Noah Claypole spies on Nancy when she reveals the secret of Oliver's identity to Rose Maylie and Mr Brownlow

River Thames 'between Southwark Bridge which is of iron, and London Bridge which is of stone'. It is very likely that this Dickensian connection was in T. S. Eliot's mind when he wrote the opening section of 'The Waste Land' in the 1920s (though he was evidently also thinking of Chaucer's Canterbury pilgrims crossing London Bridge in a fourteenth-century April). Eliot describes the habitual crowds on the bridge, and it is because of these crowds half a century earlier that Amy Dorrit prefers the relative quiet of the old iron Southwark Bridge for her meditative walks: 'If you go by the Iron Bridge … there is an escape from the noise of the street.' In Dickens's time Southwark Bridge charged a toll of 1d for a crossing, which may help to explain its lack of crowds.

Once we have crossed London Bridge we proceed up King William Street, a new street formed to serve John Rennie's 1830 bridge and named after the monarch who ceremoniously opened it. The old bridge crossed the River Thames by St Magnus-the-Martyr

'The Meeting'. George Cruikshank's illustration to *Oliver Twist* shows Noah Claypole over-hearing Nancy's evidence to Rose Maylie and Mr Brownlow on the steps leading to the river from the south side of London Bridge

Church, which stood prominently at its head (a pedestrian footpath passed underneath its tower). The church can just be glimpsed behind Adelaide House, an unlovably solid block of 1920s masonry which retains the name of an earlier building named after William IV's queen.

St Magnus lies on lower level in the now unpleasantly busy and noisy Lower Thames Street, but leading up from its tower in *Fish Street Hill* is *the Monument*, built by Sir Christopher Wren in 1671–7 in commemoration of the Great Fire of London. In *Little Dorrit* Mr F's Aunt solemnly reminds us of this fact, noting that it was 'put up after the great Fire of London … not the fire in which your Uncle George's workshops was burned down'. The Monument once stood proudly and distinctively at the point where travellers from the south entered the City, and the views from the top were once famous. Tom Pinch, lost in London in *Martin Chuzzlewit*, finds directions here and in a paved yard hard by Dickens situates Mrs Todgers's boarding house in the same novel. Otherwise, there is little left in this much redeveloped area to remind us of Dickens.

King William Street leads us to the hub of the City of London, the junction of streets in which are sited the *Mansion House*, the *Bank of England* and the old *Royal Exchange*. Dickens had no love for the lord mayors of London (nearly all of whom are characterized by pomposity and over-eating), who still reside at the Mansion House during their year of office. It is a singularly handsome building of 1739, the interiors of which are sometimes open to the public. We should turn right by the church of St Mary Woolnoth into *Lombard Street*. This street was once both commercial and residential, and has long been noted for its associations with banking (which was the occupation pursued by the medieval Lombards). At No. 2 lived the Beadnell family. George Beadnell was manager of Smith, Payne and Smith's Bank (then at No. 1). In 1830 Dickens became infatuated with George's youngest daughter, Maria. The courtship ended three years later when her parents raised objections. What their reasoning was remains undetermined. Dickens's prospects may have struck them as shaky (he was still only a junior reporter, though some commentators suspect that George may have got wind of the family's unfortunate ways with money). Maria later married Henry Winter, a London merchant. Dickens relived his passionate courtship of Maria in his account of the wooing of Dora by David Copperfield. When, in 1855, he renewed his acquaintance with the woman who had become Mrs Winter he was both shocked and amused. The garrulous, sentimental and well-endowed character of Flora Finching in *Little Dorrit* was directly inspired by her. At the height of his passion for Maria, the restless young Dickens would pace up and down Lombard Street, gazing up at her windows in the early-morning light.

It is also in Lombard Street that Dickens describes the meeting of William Dorrit, now flush with money, and the speculator Mr Merdle. In this 'golden street of the Lombards' Mr Dorrit emerges from Merdle's bank and believes he hears 'with the ears of his mind' the flattering suggestion that he is 'a wonderful man to be Mr Merdle's friend'.

The alleys that twist between Lombard Street and Cornhill retain something of a Dickensian atmosphere. Of particular significance is the now spacious *George Yard*, just beyond Wren's church of St Edmund the King. Here until 1855 stood the *George and Vulture*, where Mr Pickwick takes up residence 'in very good, old-fashioned and comfortable quarters' following Mrs Bardle's lawsuit. The buildings in George Yard are nearly all of recent construction, but if we pursue the alley straight ahead we emerge into *Castle Court* and come across the surviving stuccoed tavern now called the George and Vulture (in Dickens's time it was Thomas's Chop House, as a much-rubbed brass name-plate still indicates). This tavern, housed in three eighteenth-century properties, has a fine panelled interior and it is proud of its somewhat tenuous Pickwickian connection. Castle Court leads into *Ball Court*, which contains two tall early eighteenth-century houses knocked together as another long-established City chop-house, Simpson's. The old shop-fronts indicate that this is the type of commercial and residential property regularly associated by Dickens with slightly old-fashioned City merchants who lived 'over the shop'.

Ball Court in turn emerges into Cornhill. Hereabouts Dickens sites Scrooge's counting house and it is in the icy Cornhill that Bob Cratchit goes 'down into a slide in honour of its being Christmas Eve'. We should turn left, without sliding too conspicuously, and head for one of the entrances to Bank Station near the Royal Exchange.

Mostly *Bleak House*

I*T IS IMPORTANT to note that both Lincoln's Inn and Gray's Inn are likely to be closed to visitors at weekends. Access to the Temple is also often restricted on Saturdays and Sundays though Temple Church is regularly open for public worship.*

This itinerary runs from Holborn tube station (Central and Piccadilly lines) back to Holborn station. It is about 1½ miles.

Leave Holborn tube station into Kingsway and turn left, walking southwards. To the left we pass the Roman Catholic Church of SS *Anselm and Caecilia*. The present church was consecrated in 1909, though its façade dates only from 1951–4. The present building replaces the old Sardinian Embassy Chapel which stood to the south in Duke Street (now Sardinia Street) and which became a prime target of the anti-Catholic zeal of the Gordon Rioters in 1780. The chapel was badly damaged and its vestments and fittings were burned on a bonfire in Duke Street. The prospect of destroying the chapel is discussed by Gashford and Hugh Dennis in Chapter 50 of *Barnaby Rudge*.

Turn left at Remnant Street into *Lincoln's Inn Fields*. This historic, and still stately, open space has long been enhanced by aristocratic mansions and grand town houses, though relatively few remain intact. The large central garden, covering some 7¼ acres, was enclosed as a garden in 1734. We turn right and pass Newcastle

House, originally built in 1685–9 but substantially restored by Sir Edwin Lutyens in 1930–1. Much more indicative of the old glories of the fields is Nos. 59–60, Lindsey House, built in 1639–41 and often attributed to Inigo Jones. For Dickensians, however, the prime interest of this part of Lincoln's Inn Fields lies in the neighbouring pair of houses, Nos. 57–58, built in a similar style in about 1730. No. 58 was the residence of Dickens's intimate friend, and future biographer, John Forster. Here in early December 1844 Dickens read his newly completed Christmas book, *The Chimes*, to a party of his close male friends, producing (according to the artist Daniel Maclise, who drew the scene) both 'shrieks of laughter' and 'floods of tears'. This is the house that Dickens allots to the lawyer Mr Tulkinghorn in *Bleak House*. It is described as 'a large house, formerly a house of state … let off in sets of chambers … and in those shrunken fragments of its greatness, lawyers lie like maggots in nuts'. Neither

Charles Dickens Museum

John Forster's House, Lincoln's Inn Fields, *c*. 1900. Here Dickens read *The Chimes* to a circle of close friends in 1844. This seems to be the house that Dickens gives to Mr Tulkinghorn in *Bleak House*, though it has no allegorical painted ceiling

Lindsay House nor its neighbours possess the allegorical painted ceiling which Dickens makes much of in his novel.

If we continue southwards and turn briefly out of the Fields into *Portsmouth Street* we encounter a slightly surprising relic of old London – a timber-framed building dated 1567. This is the so-called Old Curiosity Shop 'immortalized by Charles Dickens'. The claim that this is the actual Old Curiosity Shop flies in the face of Dickens's statement in the novel of that name that the shop had been 'long ago pulled down'. The present associations with Dickens seem to date only from the period after the novelist's death. The very survival of the building may, however, be due to its false claim to literary note. It is also the last reminder of the many lost wooden buildings that once stood nearby in the area of Wych Street and which were cleared away during the construction of Kingsway and the Aldwych in the opening years of the twentieth century.

We turn back into Lincolns Inn Fields and continue right, walking along the south side. Here, with a prominent portico, is the *Royal College of Surgeons*, originally built here in the opening years of the nineteenth century and reconstructed in 1835–6 (it was badly altered and expanded in 1888 and 1937). When Richard Carstone considers becoming a ship's surgeon in Chapter 13 of *Bleak House*, Mr Boythorn characteristically explodes into a diatribe against the Admiralty Board and 'similar gatherings of jolter-headed clods', suggesting that their necks should be wrung and their skulls arranged in Surgeons' Hall. A modern visitor in search of the kind of macabre relics once instructively shown to medical students would do well to visit the excellent Hunterian Museum, which is open to the public in part of the college.

We continue along the south side of Lincoln's Inn Fields. Facing us on the east side is *Lincoln's Inn*. (If Lincoln's Inn is shut at weekends, turn right into Serle Street to Carey Street and resume the walk there.) The present gate to Lincoln's Inn from the Fields forms part of the redevelopment of 1842–5. To the right lie the new hall and the library, both grandly designed in the neo-Tudor style by Philip Hardwick. Visitors should walk straight ahead into New Square, a wonderful surviving complex of red-brick late seventeenth-century houses surrounding a green lawn. The houses were designed to be divided up into chambers and to provide accommodation for resident members of the inn. The whole is more reminiscent of a campus like that of Harvard than of an ancient English university. We will return to the square after pressing forward to the *chapel* and the *old hall*. The chapel was rebuilt in 1619–23 and has a splendid, vaulted open under-croft in the late-Gothic style, which once provided a public space where lawyers could talk, negotiate or meet clients. The old hall lies to the south, and was built in 1489–94. It is not particularly distin-guished from an architectural point of view, and it is rarely open for public inspection, but it contains a large and singularly dull painting by Hogarth of St Paul before Felix. For Dickensians it has special significance as the setting for the session of the Court of Chancery with which *Bleak House* opens (the court would sit here as an alter-native to Westminster Hall). Behind the hall is Old Square,

Old Square, Lincoln's Inn, c. 1890. Much of this sixteenth-century range survives, but this photograph beautifully evokes the atmosphere of the opening chapters of *Bleak House*. Kenge and Carboy have their offices here

where the solicitors Kenge and Carboy have their offices in the same novel. Esther Summerson describes 'a silent square' and an 'old nook in the corner, where there was an entrance up a steep, broad flight of stairs, like an entrance to a church'. From the windows she also gloomily notes the existence of a real churchyard with gravestones (these have now disappeared). Through the foggy gloom Esther is conducted into the stately presence of the Lord Chancellor somewhere off a passage out of Old Square. It is in the Lord Chancellor's chambers that she first encounters Richard Carstone and Ada Clare.

We can leave the cramped old square via the covered passage containing the hall doors. We pass the seventeenth-century Old Buildings and emerge again into the elegant spaciousness of New Square. We proceed down the east side of the square to the passage facing us and emerge into Carey Street, where we are immediately

Temple Bar, Strand, shortly before its removal in 1878. Beyond it we can glimpse the church of St Clement Danes and Fleet Street

confronted by the northern flank of G. E. Street's great Law Courts or Royal Courts of Justice, constructed here in 1871–82. The site was covered in Dickens's time by what was deemed to be untidy slum property. Dividing the Strand from Fleet Street stood Temple Bar, the removal of which was vital to Street's scheme. After the unification of the Common Law and Chancery departments, the old courts, which had anciently sat at Westminster Hall and adjoining court buildings, were removed here, thus rendering many of the bitter asides in *Bleak House* redundant. The complex Strand façade of the Law Courts is of stone, but the Carey Street elevation is of mixed red brick and stone, a style sometimes irreverently known in Victorian times as 'streaky bacon' (interestingly enough the epithet was used in quite another context by Dickens when referring to his intermixture of comedy and tragedy in *Oliver Twist*).

The construction of Street's courts completely altered the nature of *Bell Yard*, down which we now proceed. It is no longer a 'yard',

Bell Yard, Fleet Street, *c.* 1860. Bell Yard is now little more than a passage at the eastern side of the Royal Courts of Justice. In rooms above a chandler's shop in this 'narrow alley' Esther Summerson discovers the neglected Neckett children in Chapter 15 of *Bleak House*

but a passage leading us into Fleet Street. Bell Yard is described by Dickens as 'a narrow alley' and is the title of Chapter 15 of *Bleak House*. It is here that he sites the chandler's shop above which live the orphaned Neckett children (who are discovered here by Esther Summerson). Halfway down, Bell Yard becomes Andrews Crosse.

We emerge into Fleet Street. If we look to the left there stands in the middle of the road the column marking the division between the City of London and the City of Westminster and between the square mile of territory administered by the Lord Mayor and Corporation of London and the amorphous mass of the rest of London. The column which is crowned with the City's heraldic emblem, a griffin, stands on the site once occupied by what Dickens called a 'leaden-headed old obstruction' – *Temple Bar*. On the Fleet Street side, and overshadowed by the bar, he situates Tellson's Bank in *A Tale of Two Cities*. This handsome gate, which was not generally admired by Victorian Londoners, was taken down in 1878 and rebuilt as a monstrous garden ornament on an estate in Hertfordshire. It was returned to London in the opening years of the twenty-first century and now stands to the north of St Paul's Cathedral.

We cross Fleet Street and enter the Temple, which faces us, via *Middle Temple Lane*. Suddenly we leave the noise of a major thoroughfare for a by-way, blessedly free of traffic. The narrow Middle Temple Lane is immediately redolent of Dickens's London, with its overhanging seventeenth- and eighteenth-century buildings and its semi-collegiate air of being cut off from London's habitual money-grubbing. We emerge into Essex and Brick Courts to the right, where, despite severe bomb damage during the Second World War, the rebuilding still manages to convey a good sense of architectural harmony. We pass through the arch facing us, dated 1677, and enter New Court and beyond it *Fountain Court*, with its fine lamp standards and its mature trees. The present fountain dates only from 1975, but its sound permeates this extraordinarily pleasant corner of historic London. Fountain Court and *Garden Court* beyond it are memorably described in *Great Expectations* (see Chapter 3), for Pip and Herbert Pocket have chambers 'at the top of the last house' in the old Garden Court which lay to the south of where we are standing (the present Garden Court dates only from 1884–5). As Dickens explains, the

Temple of *Great Expectations* was much more exposed to bad weather rolling in up the Thames from the North Sea. This was the period before the Embankment was constructed. The wild weather of *Great Expectations* perfectly reflects the disconcerting atmosphere of the strained encounter between Pip and Magwitch (who has returned illicitly from Australia). Infinitely more benign weather shines on the tryst between Ruth Pinch and John Westlock which takes place by the fountain in *Fountain Court* in *Martin Chuzzlewit*.

The non-Dickensian literary associations of this part of Middle Temple are complex, and Dickens himself would have been particularly aware of Shakespeare's links to the gardens (the Wars of the Roses are reputed to have begun here as Yorkists and Lancastrians plucked white and red roses) and to *Middle Temple Hall* (where *Twelfth Night* was performed by Shakespeare's company). We pass the wonderful hall as we turn left through Garden Court. We recross Middle Temple Lane and enter the Inner Temple via the arch facing us.

Middle Temple Hall, 1827. This engraving by Thomas H. Shepherd shows the great sixteenth-century Hall of the Inn as Dickens would have known it. The additions to the east side of the Hall have been substantially reconstructed since damage in the Second World War

Much of the historical architecture of the Inner Temple vanished during the Second World War (this was a clear target on moonlit nights for bombers following the Thames). Elm Court and Pump Court are attractive enough, but virtually every building is a polite neo-Georgian reconstruction of the 1950s. Inner Temple Hall was destroyed in 1940 and was rebuilt in a singularly dull manner in 1955.

If we go up the short flight of steps we reach *Temple Church*, which flanks the hall in a pleasant open square (Church Court). The church was very badly damaged in the bombing in 1941 and was restored in 1947–57, a drastic reconstruction which removed all traces of the systematic nineteenth-century 'restorations' of 1825–30, 1841–3 and 1862 (which produced the interiors which Dickens would have known). It is an extraordinary building still, despite the ravages of time, fire, bombs and architects, but Dickens seems to take it and its long history for granted in his novels.

If we walk straight ahead through the arch between Inner Temple

Church Court, The Temple, *c.* 1870. This photograph shows the Master's House (destroyed in the Second World War and since rebuilt). This is the 'dismal churchyard' onto which Mortimer Lightwood's chambers look in *Our Mutual Friend*. The tomb slab in the foreground is that of Oliver Goldsmith, moved here in 1860

Library and the Francis Taylor Building we enter the finest surviving ranges of Inner Temple known as King's Bench Walk. To the right is the stone-faced Mitre Court of 1830 but facing us, and stretching down to the Embankment, is a very handsome range of red-brick terraced houses, most of which date from the late seventeenth century. King's Bench Walk often appears in films and on television as a 'representative' eighteenth- or nineteenth-century London street. To the right of King's Bench Walk Buildings and facing it on the west side is *Paper Building*. The present neo-Tudor brick building dates only from 1838 (extended in 1847–8), replacing the building in which Sir John Chester has his chambers in *Barnaby Rudge* and Mr Stryver his in *A Tale of Two Cities*.

We retrace our steps back to Church Court and turn right at Temple Church, passing by its fine Romanesque west doorway. To the left is Dr Johnson's Building of 1857–8 and beyond the Church is Goldsmith's Building of 1861. The names commemorate two notable eighteenth-century residents. If we turn right in front of Goldsmith's Chambers we see the remains of the old burying ground where there is a monument covering Oliver Goldsmith's tomb (Goldsmith was a favourite writer of Dickens's). This is the part of the Inner Temple which figures so memorably in *Our Mutual Friend*. Mortimer Lightwood and Eugene Wrayburn have chambers in the building that preceded the present Goldsmith's Building. It had 'dismal windows' commanding a view of the 'dismal churchyard'. Outside the chambers, by the gate into Fleet Street, Bradley Headstone hovers nightly, malevolently waiting for Eugene to leave the Temple. We leave it via the same gateway and cross Fleet Street. Looking back we can see that Inner Temple Gate is surmounted by the impressive timbered structure of 1610–11 containing the great chamber known as Prince Henry's Room.

We proceed northwards along Chancery Lane. To the right, in Fleet Street, is the church of *St Dunstan-in-the-West*, which is octagon-shaped, and was rebuilt 1830–3. It has a tower surmounted by a stylish octagonal lantern and a fine bracketed clock (which only came back to the church in 1935). This clock is noted by David Copperfield, but the tower and its consoling bells figure prominently in Dickens's second Christmas book, *The Chimes*. Next

The Hall of Clifford's Inn, 1827. Engraving by Thomas H. Shepherd

to St Dunstan's, up a short alley, is a desultory gateway which forms the only surviving part of *Clifford's Inn*. Tip Dorrit worked in chambers there, and in the alley leading to what Dickens describes as a 'mouldy little plantation, or cat-preserve', Mr Boffin offers the post of secretary to Rokesmith in *Our Mutual Friend*.

Returning to Chancery Lane we pass first, on our right, the site of *Serjeant's Inn* (demolished in 1910). In Chapter 19 of *Bleak House* Dickens describes the Temple, Chancery Lane, Serjeant's Inn, and Lincoln's Inn when the courts are not sitting as being like 'tidal harbours at low water; where stranded proceedings, offices at anchor, idle clerks lounging on top-sided stools ... lie high and dry upon some ooze of the long vacation'. Beyond the site is the former Public Record Office (now part of King's College). This substantial building, in a bland Gothic style, was begun in 1851 and added to until 1896. It was designed to resist fire, with iron doors, brick arches and cast-iron roof-tiles. The outstanding collection of historic records was moved to new premises at Kew in 1997.

We are now solidly in 'legal London'. To the right is the Law

Cliffords's Inn, c. 1900. This photograph shows mirrors suspended under windows to direct light upwards into shady chambers. This was a common enough phenomenon in Dickens's London but has all but disappeared today

Charles Dickens Museum

Society of 1829–32 (extended in 1848–50 and 1856–7). The physical growth of the building is indicative not only of the new regulation of the profession but also of the enhanced social position of solicitors during the nineteenth century. Beyond Carey Street we begin to skirt the outer reaches of Lincoln's Inn. On the corner of *Chichester Rents* once stood the *Old Ship Tavern*, probably the original of the Sol's Arms, where the inquest on Nemo takes place in *Bleak House*. Here too was Krook's Rag and Bottle Warehouse, where Nemo and Miss Flite have lodgings in the same novel. It is described by Dickens as a 'narrow back street … blinded by the wall of Lincoln's Inn', though Miss Flite, who lives at the top of the building, is delighted by her glimpse of the roof of the old hall of the inn, where the Court of Chancery sits. Chichester Rents is still narrow but it is now so completely reconstructed, and so respectable, that its seedy Dickensian associations seem remote. Beyond is the rebuilt gate of Lincoln's Inn, through which Esther Summerson passes into the 'silent square' containing Kenge and Carboy's offices.

Crossing back to the right side of Chancery Lane and briefly retracing our steps, we come to *Breams Buildings* which marks the site of Symond's Inn, 'a little, pale, wall-eyed, woe-begone inn, like a large dust-bin of two compartments and a sifter', where Mr Vholes has his chambers in *Bleak House*. Symond's Inn was demolished in 1873.

We turn right off Chancery Lane into Cursitor Street and then left again into *Took's Court*. This is the street thinly disguised by Dickens as Cook's Court. Here Mr Snagsby has his law stationer's shop in *Bleak House*. The court is described as 'a shady place'. Despite war-time bombing some old houses survive, and No. 15, now called Dickens House, is the building most likely to be the original of Snagsby's shop. At the end of Took's Court we turn right and then left into Furnival Street and continue ahead to Holborn.

The Courtyard of Barnard's Inn, *c.* 1870. The Inn was demolished in 1910, but this photograph reminds us both of the once sequestered nature of the decaying inn and of the kind of accommodation it once provided

Here we turn right and look for the courtyard entrance to *Barnard's Inn* at numbers 20–23 (the miniature hall of the inn now forms part of Gresham College). The Mercers' Company bought the premises for their school in 1892, and much of the site was redeveloped in 1991–2. Pip has chambers in the old inn on first coming to London in *Great Expectations*.

We can continue walking eastward for a few minutes towards the now inconsequential site of *Thavies Inn*. St Andrew Street cut across part of its site in the 1860s but a row of eighteenth-century houses survived off Holborn until the Second World War (Thavies Inn House roughly marks where it was). This 'narrow street of high houses' is said by Mr Guppy to be 'no distance' from Kenge and Carboy's at Lincoln's Inn. Here was Mrs Jellyby's house where Esther finds the youngest Jellyby with his head stuck in the area railings.

Retracing our steps to the top of Furnival Street we should look across to the other side of Holborn. Here in its red terracotta splendour stands the Gothic former Prudential Assurance Building by Alfred Waterhouse. This stands on the site of the ancient *Furnival's Inn*, where Dickens had chambers from 1834 to 1837. The inn itself had been reconstructed in the first quarter of the nineteenth century after the Society had been dissolved in 1817. Dickens describes it in *Martin Chuzzlewit* as 'a shady, quiet place, echoing to the footsteps of the stragglers who have business there' and as 'rather monotonous and gloomy on summer evenings'. This structure was in turn replaced in 1879 by the first part of Waterhouse's building, which was considerably extended between 1899 and 1906.

On the south side of Holborn, if we continue walking westwards, we come to the far more redolent *Staple Inn*. On the Holborn side the inn has a much-restored rambling half-timbered façade which in Dickens's time was concealed by stucco. The inn ceased functioning as a legal society in the latter half of the nineteenth century and was sold in 1884. It was restored by the Prudential Assurance Company in the 1880s and was severely damaged by bombs in 1944. Nevertheless, it is the most complete and enchanting of the old inns of Chancery. It serves today as offices and accommodation for the Institute of Actuaries. Here, the lawyer, Mr Grewgious, has his chambers in *Edwin Drood*. Dickens describes it in the novel as 'two irregular quadrangles' and as 'one of those nooks where a few smoky sparrows twitter in the smoky trees … It is one of those nooks which are legal nooks.' Behind the façade are two courtyards, a hall and a garden, which despite some bland post-war rebuilding, still convey much of the charm of Dickens's 'legal nook'.

We return to Holborn and cross the road. Gray's Inn Road leads off to the north, but we continue westward to the gate of Gray's Inn, which stands just before the extraordinary stone façade of the Citie of Yorke public house (formerly Henekey's, and built only in 1923–4). The gatehouse of Gray's Inn is a modern reconstruction and it leads into a somewhat nondescript passage. We go straight on and enter *South Square* where, alas, most of the buildings are relatively modern following severe damage in the Second World War. In Dickens's day much of this was Holborn Square, where at No. 5 (now the surviving No. 1 South Square) were the offices of Ellis and Blackmore where Dickens began work as a clerk in a 'poor old set of chambers of three rooms'. Holborn Square is where Traddles has his chambers in *David Copperfield* and Dickens's descriptions of it both in the novel and in his essay 'Chambers' of 1860 are singularly unflattering.

We continue past the hall into *Gray's Inn Square* where much more of historic interest survives (though there is little that is comparable to the stately attractiveness of New Square at Lincoln's Inn). Turn left into Field Court and then right into *Raymond Buildings* which were built in 1825. Here on the second floor of No. 1 (now a reconstruction) were the chambers to which Ellis and Blackmore moved early in 1828. Dickens left their employ in November of that year and took away with him a distinct distaste for lawyers and their ways. He was, however, fond enough of the fine gardens which lie behind Raymond Buildings to refer to them in *Little Dorrit* as the place where Arthur Clennam once courted Flora Finching. When Dickens took up residence in *Doughty Street* in 1837 he too must have availed himself of this fine open space with its tall trees and spacious lawns.

If you have the energy, a visit to the *Charles Dickens Museum* is highly recommended. Dickens lived at 48 Doughty Street from March 1837 until the end of 1839. Here he finished *Pickwick Papers* and wrote *Oliver Twist* and *Nicholas Nickleby*. It is now his only surviving major residence in London and the museum contains outstanding relics of the novelist and his art. Doughty Street can be reached from Gray's Inn by walking up Jockey's Fields by the side of Raymond Buildings to the gate on Theobald's Road. Turn right and cross the road beyond Holborn Library and turn left into John Street which leads into Doughty Street. No. 48 is on the right-hand side. To return to the underground from Doughty Street, retrace your steps to Theobald's Road and turn right into Gray's Inn Road. Chancery Lane station (Central Line) is at the junction with Holborn.

If you want to proceed immediately to Holborn station, return to High Holborn via Gray's Inn Gatehouse and turn right. Cross High Holborn and walk towards Kingsway.

Mostly *Oliver Twist*

THIS WALK MOVES southwards through Islington to the western parts of the City of London. It begins at Angel tube station (Northern Line: Bank Branch) and ends at St Paul's tube station (Central Line). It is about 2 miles.

Emerging from Angel tube station into *Islington High Street*, cross the road and turn left. At No. 11 is the building that was once the *Peacock Inn* (it is marked with a plaque). The Peacock public house closed in 1962 but there was a long-established coaching inn on the site and it is here that the Yorkshire-bound coach bearing Nicholas Nickleby, Squeers and Squeers's unhappy pupils stops in Chapter 5 of *Nicholas Nickleby*. Dickens also mentions the Peacock in his Christmas story 'The Holly Tree', and describes the frozen coach travellers warming themselves up with 'hot purl in self-preservation' ('purl' was a flavoured hot beer mixed with gin).

On the corner of Pentonville Road was the old Angel Inn, from which the area takes its name. We turn right into Pentonville Road and walk westward, crossing Penton, Cynthia and Rodney Streets. At what is now 154 Pentonville Road was St James's Church, built in 1787–8 and demolished in 1981. Its pretty façade survives, though the body of the building is now residential. To the side, with an entrance in Rodney Street, is the former churchyard, now *Joseph Grimaldi Park*. Facing the entrance gate is the restored grave of the great pantomime clown Joseph Grimaldi (who died in 1837). Dickens was commissioned by the publisher Bentley to 'edit'

St James's Church, Clerkenwell, *c.* 1900. The church of 1788–92 is seen here hemmed in by the kind of buildings described as 'narrow dirty streets', in *Our Mutual Friend*

Charles Dickens Museum

Grimaldi's *Memoirs* in 1838. They appeared in two volumes, edited by 'Boz' and with illustrations by George Cruikshank. It was largely hack work on Dickens's part.

Cross over Pentonville Road, and turn left, back towards the Angel but on the south side of the road. At Claremont Square turn right. The west side of the square leads into *Amwell Street*. This was land developed by the New River Company in the 1820s and the houses on Claremont Square still face on to a covered reservoir. At 71 Amwell Street a plaque marks the house lived in by Dickens's sometime friend and illustrator George Cruikshank (1792–1878). Cruikshank, who provided the particularly brilliant engravings for *Sketches by 'Boz'* and *Oliver Twist*, lived in this newly built house between 1824 and 1849. It was perhaps the most creative period of his life. His friendship with Dickens cooled in the 1840s when the artist espoused a 'fanatic' teetotalism. As an old man, he falsely claimed to have provided much of the plot-line and characters of *Oliver Twist*.

His house is, perhaps, the kind of respectable house in the Pentonville area that we can imagine Mr Brownlow occupying in *Oliver Twist*, though for those readers who believe that Brownlow merits something larger and more becoming his middle-class status one of the houses round the corner in *Myddleton Square* might seem more becoming. It was built in 1824–7. In the middle of the square is the brick Gothic Church of St Mark (1826–8). We walk round the square and leave it by Chadwell Street, which leads eastward behind the church (the street to our right, now called *Arlington Way*, is the 'small street which terminates at Saddler's Wells Theatre' mentioned in Chapter 8 of *Oliver Twist*). We can either turn down here or carry on to *St John Street* and turn right. This is a surviving part of the route into London taken by Oliver Twist and the Dodger as they descend from Islington to Fagin's den near Saffron Hill. St John's Street becomes Rosebery Avenue, the construction of which in the late nineteenth century demolished many of the slum properties familiar to Dickens.

Immediately to the right in Rosebery Avenue is *Sadler's Wells Theatre*. The first theatre on the site was constructed in 1683, but the present building dates from 1996–8. The theatre that Dickens knew was built in the mid-eighteenth century and reconstructed in 1844. It was in many ways typical of the large number of suburban theatres of the time, combining popular dramatic entertainments with the attractions of a music hall and a beer garden (at one point it boasted an interior tank, allowing it to host aquatic spectacles). It was here that Joseph Grimaldi gave his last performance in March 1828.

Continuing southwards down Rosebery Avenue we pass to the right, New River Head, the reservoirs and the site of the former headquarters of the New River Company. The Metropolitan Water Board built its new offices here in 1914–20 (now flats). We cross Rosebery Avenue, turn left down Garnault Street and cross Rosomon Street. To the right is Exmouth Market, formerly Exmouth Street, which leads into *Farringdon Road* (which Dickens knew as Coppice Row and down which the Dodger and Oliver walk). We continue straight ahead across the small Spa Fields park. As the name implies, there was a pleasure garden here in the eighteenth century, but the present park replaces a disused burial ground (the rest of the area was redeveloped in the 1930s as part of a systematic process of slum clearance initiated by the former Finsbury Borough Council). We turn into Clerkenwell Close and ahead we can glimpse the late eighteenth-century spire of St James's, Clerkenwell. We continue past the church, which was built 1788–92, and eventually emerge into Clerkenwell Green. In Chapter 10 of *Oliver Twist* Dickens rudely describes 'an open square in Clerkenwell which is yet called, by some strange perversion of terms "The Green"'. Eighteenth-century Clerkenwell is the suburban residence of Gabriel Varden in *Barnaby Rudge* and of Jarvis Lorry in *A Tale of Two Cities*. By the mid-nineteenth century the area had become known for its concentration of jewellers' and watchmakers' shops. It is here, amongst 'the poorer shops of small retail traders in commodities to eat and drink and keep folks warm, and of Italian frame-makers, and of barbers, and of brokers, and of dealers in dogs and singing-birds', that Silas Wegg visits Mr Venus's taxidermist's shop in *Our Mutual Friend*. Venus's shop is in a 'narrow and dirty street' though his original appears to have inhabited St Martin's Lane.

Only a few pre-nineteenth-century domestic buildings now survive amid the winding alleys which characterize the area, but the green is still graced on its west side by the fine façade of the former *Middlesex Sessions House* (1779–82). The old building was altered 1859–60 and again after 1876. It was to the Sessions House that Bumble makes his way in Chapter 17 of *Oliver Twist*.

We continue down Clerkenwell Road and cross Farringdon Road (which follows the valley of the old River Fleet). In Dickens's time Coppice Lane changed its name to Victoria Street at this junction. We continue along Clerkenwell Road, turn left into Onslow Street, and walk down the steps in front of us. Onslow Street ends at Saffron Street, where we turn right and then left into Saffron Hill. In Dickens's time Saffron Hill ran from Field Lane to Vine Street, but despite these rustic-sounding names, the Saffron Hill area was a notorious and squalid slum in the first half of the nineteenth century. As even the present ups and downs in the topography suggest, this was a low-lying and once insalubrious area on the west bank of the heavily polluted River Fleet. For its criminal inhabitants its main advantage lay in the fact that if the police came in at

Charles Dickens Museum

Clerkenwell Sessions House, Clerkenwell Green, 1805. The Middlesex Sessions House of 1779–82 replaced a Jacobean building known as Hicks's Hall, named after its founder, Sir Baptist Hicks. The building was enlarged in 1860–76

Little Saffron Hill, c. 1896. The buildings in the foreground would have been familiar to Dickens. In the background, however, we can glimpse newly built working-class flats

the front door, suspects could escape via back exits leading onto a maze of alleys and rickety bridges over the dirty river. We have literally descended to this point. When a now long-disappeared church (St Peter's) was built here in 1832, the neighbourhood was described as being 'sunk in ignorance and vice of the saddest character'. One commentator noted that the clergy, when visiting their parish, were obliged to be accompanied by a plain-clothes policeman!

In *Oliver Twist* Dickens describes Oliver's arrival at a 'very narrow and dirty' street, the air of which was 'impregnated with filthy odours'. At the bottom of the hill, like some lurking beast's lair, lies Fagin's den. It is hard to imagine it now, even on a wretched, grey winter's day, for there has been much rebuilding since the reconstruction work associated with Holborn Viaduct in the late 1860s. Nowadays we are surrounded by office blocks and Field Lane has

Charles Dickens Museum

Viaduct Chambers, Saffron Hill, Holborn, 1896. This building was sometimes identified with Fagin's den. It has long disappeared

229

been obliterated. Nevertheless, this is the site of Oliver Twist's nightmarish time in Fagin's thrall, and original readers of the novel would probably have been familiar with the area's dark reputation as a resort of the criminal underclass.

When we reach Greville Street (formerly Charles Street) we turn left and turn into what is left of *Bleeding Heart Yard*. This is an enclave of late Victorian industrial buildings which now house a selection of wine bars and restaurants. It was very different when Dickens selected it as the decidedly shabby residence of the Plornish family and the location of Daniel Doyce's factory in *Little Dorrit*. It was then approached 'down a flight of steps … and got out of by a low gate-way into a maze of shabby streets'.

We retrace our steps to Saffron Hill and go up the stairs at the end which lead us into Charterhouse Street. Here we turn right, and on our right is Ely Place, a far more genteel enclave of houses than Bleeding Heart Yard could ever have been. The gates, which survive, kept poor London just about at bay. The street was laid out in 1773 on the site of the Bishop of Ely's medieval palace. The palace's lovely chapel survives as St Etheldreda's Church. This served as a Welsh chapel until 1873 when it was acquired for Roman Catholic use and extensively restored. If we turn left down the alley before we reach the church we find the eighteenth-century public house called the Mitre (like St Etheldreda's, it is well worth a visit, though it has no particular Dickensian associations). The alley emerges into Hatton Garden where, under a 'low archway' at No. 54, once stood the 'very notorious Metropolitan Police Office presided over by Mr Fang' to which Oliver Twist is brought after his arrest and from which he is rescued by Mr Brownlow. 'Mr Fang' was very closely modelled on a magistrate called Laing who served here from 1836 to 1838, and whose attitude to 'summary justice' was closely observed by Dickens.

We turn left in Hatton Garden and emerge at Holborn Circus. Opposite us is the site of Thavies Inn (see Itinerary Two). We turn left and, crossing Charterhouse Street, turn into Holborn Viaduct. If we cross over the road we arrive at *St Andrew's Holborn*, reconstructed by Sir Christopher Wren in 1684–6, gutted by bombing in 1941 and reconsecrated in 1961. The church is often open and

The former Police Office, Hatton Wall, *c.* 1896. The site of the 'very notorious Metropolitan Police Office' presided over by Mr Fang in *Oliver Twist*. It is in fact the former Hatton Garden Police Court presided over by A.S. Laing in the years 1836–8

Charles Dickens Museum

inside, under its tower, is the tomb of Captain Coram, the benevolent founder of the Foundling Hospital. 'Tattycoram', the unhappy orphan adopted by the Meagles family in *Little Dorrit*, is patronizingly named after him.

Holborn Viaduct was London's first, and grandest, overpass, built in 1863–9 in order to relieve the problematic and muddy dip into the Fleet valley at *Holborn Hill* (which is described in the opening chapter of *Bleak House*). The viaduct is in fact a handsome cast-iron bridge spanning Farringdon Street. At each corner once stood stone-faced office blocks decorated with statues of London worthies. Two survive.

If we cross the viaduct to its north side and continue eastward we reach *Snow Hill*, which leads off to the left. Here stood the Saracen's Head Inn 'its portals guarded by two Saracens' heads and shoulders'. It is here that Mr Squeers bases himself during his sojourns in London. The old inn was demolished in 1868. Just beyond Snow

Holborn Bridge, 1827. This engraving by Thomas H. Shepherd suggests something of the dip down into the valley of the River Fleet and the inconvenience it once caused to traffic. This is the muddy Holborn Hill of the opening of *Bleak House*

Newgate Prison, 1805

Hill is *St Sepulchre's Church*, whose fine but much-restored fifteenth-century tower contains the clock that once announced the hour of executions in Newgate Prison on the other side of the road. Dickens mentions the dire summons in *Barnaby Rudge*.

We cross the road and turn down Old Bailey. The *Central Criminal Court*, which stretches round the corner of Newgate Street and Old Bailey, stands on the site of the old Newgate Prison and its adjoining Sessions House. Both buildings made a deep, lasting and dark impression on Dickens, and are both described in Chapter 3. The prison and court were demolished at the very end of the nineteenth century, despite a vigorous campaign to save the superb rusticated blank wall of the prison building. The new Central Criminal Court replaced it in 1900–7 (with an extension of 1970–2). In *Old Bailey* itself was London's pillory (last used in 1830) and, after executions had ceased at Tyburn, public hangings took place from November 1783 to May 1868. Here Fagin dies at the very end of *Oliver Twist*. When Oliver and Mr Brownlow emerge from the prison in Chapter 52 day is dawning and they note the neighbouring windows 'were filled with people, smoking and playing cards to beguile the time; the crowd were pushing, quarrelling, and joking'. In the middle of the street, however, is 'the black stage, the crossbeam, the rope, and all the hideous apparatus of death'.

Continuing along Old Bailey we emerge at the bottom into *Ludgate Hill* with St Paul's to the left and Ludgate Circus to the right. At 42 Ludgate Hill was the London Coffee House at a window of which Arthur Clennam sits on the dreary Sunday evening of his return to London in Chapter 3 of the first part of *Little Dorrit*. It is a 'gloomy, close and stale' evening and Arthur disconsolately listens to the chiming church bells (one of which must be that of the neighbouring St Martin's, a Wren church that escaped damage in the Second World War). Arthur looks out on 'the dull houses opposite' (all of which have now been rebuilt), and when the rain begins to fall he stares at the people sheltering 'under cover of the passage opposite'. We should cross Ludgate Hill and seek out one such 'passage', *Pilgrim Street*. Turning left, and then right, this should take us into *Carter Lane*, from which we turn off right into *Wardrobe Place*. All of the alleys off Carter Lane have some historic interest, and many contain a good selection of old City domestic and commercial architecture, but Wardrobe Place is special. It has no particular Dickens connection, but it is a rare survival and it readily brings to mind the many quiet courtyards which were once so much a feature of the City. This is the kind of backwater where Scrooge lives or where the Cheerybles have their offices. It is surrounded by eighteenth- and nineteenth-century buildings and it is shaded by mature trees.

We emerge again into Carter Lane and turn right up *Dean's Court*. Here once stood *Doctors' Commons*, in 'a very old nook near Saint Paul's Churchyard ... a little out-of-the-way place ... that has an ancient monopoly in suits about people's wills and people's

Ludgate Street and St Paul's Cathedral, c. 1850. This calotype photograph captures much of the atmosphere of Arthur Clennam's sojourn in the London Coffee House at 42 Ludgate Hill in *Little Dorrit* (this is the Family Hotel shown in the photograph). Despite the quietness of the streets this may not be a Sunday (as the shades suggest that businesses are about to open), but it certainly evokes a London 'gloomy, close and stale'

marriages'. It and its working are described in Chapter 23 of *David Copperfield*. The courts housed here ceased to function in the late 1850s and the buildings were demolished in 1867. On the left further up Dean's Court, however, is the old *Deanery* of St Paul's (now the Bishop of London's residence). This is the finest surviving seventeenth-century mansion in the City of London and, like Wardrobe Place, it can serve to remind us of the many similar buildings that were steadily demolished and replaced by office blocks in the latter half of the nineteenth century. Although it stands proudly and elegantly without the need of wooden stays and props, it may remind some readers of the creaking Clennam house in Lower Thames Street in *Little Dorrit*.

We emerge from Dean's Court into St Paul's Churchyard, cross the road in front of the cathedral and turn left on the north side of the church. This part of the pedestrianized churchyard is now flanked by the rebuilt Temple Bar, removed here in the opening years of the twenty-first century (see Chapter 3 and Itinerary Two). If we turn left at the end of the churchyard and cross Paternoster Row we reach St Paul's underground station.

Further Reading

THERE HAVE BEEN many good and useful books written about Dickens and London. They began to appear soon after the author's death, when much of the London that he knew was still undemolished, unbombed and unredeveloped. They have been followed by a steady stream of volumes which have come to terms with the often drastic changes in street architecture and urban topography. The ones I have selected as further reading are a mere handful, but each of them offers a distinctive insight and all of them have been of particular use to me. I have included several now rare Victorian guidebooks to London, which are particularly informative if they can be tracked down. There is also no reason to suppose that the volumes published in the first half of the twentieth century are in any way redundant as sources of information and pleasure.

Ackroyd, Peter, 'Introduction' to *Dickens' London: An Imaginative Vision* (Headline, London, 1987)

Allbut, Robert, *London Rambles 'En Zigzag' with Charles Dickens* (Edward Curtice, London, 1886)

Anon, *The London of Charles Dickens* (London Transport Executive, London, 1970)

Anon, *Charles Dickens and Southwark* (The London Borough of Southwark, London, 1974, revised 1994)

Bohn, Henry G. (ed.), *The Pictorial Handbook of London, Comprising its Antiquities, Architecture, Arts, Manufactures, Trade, Social, Literary and Scientific Institutions, Exhibitions and Galleries of Art etc.* (Henry G. Bohn, London, 1854)

Chancellor, E. Beresford, *The London of Charles Dickens: Being an*

Account of the Haunts of his Characters and the Topographical setting of his Novels (Grant Richards, London, 1924)

Cunningham, Peter, *A Hand-Book of London: Past and Present* (John Murray, London, 1850)

Dexter, Walter, *The London of Charles Dickens* (Cecil Palmer, London, 1923)

Hare, Augustus, J.C., *Walks in London* (George Allen, London, 1901)

Matz, B.W., *Dickensian Inns and Taverns*, 2nd edn (Cecil Palmer, London, 1923)

Moretti, Franco, *Atlas of the European Novel 1800–1900* (Verso, London and New York, 1998)

Stamp, Gavin, *The Changing Metropolis: Earliest Photographs of London 1839–1879* (Viking, Harmondsworth, 1984)

Timbs, John, *Curiosities of London: Exhibiting the Most Rare and Remarkable Objects of Interest in the Metropolis* (London, David Bogue, 1855)

Weinreb, Ben and Hibbert, Christopher, *The London Encyclopaedia* (London, Macmillan, 1983)

Willey, Russ, *London Gazetteer* (Chambers Harrap, Edinburgh, 2006)

Index